Five-Minute Activities

CAMBRIDGE HANDBOOKS FOR LANGUAGE TEACHERS
General Editor: Michael Swan

This is a series of practical guides for teachers of English and other languages. Illustrative examples are usually drawn from the field of English as a foreign or second language, but the ideas and techniques described can equally well be used in the teaching of any language.

In this series:

Drama Techniques in Language Learning – A resource book of communication activities for language teachers
by Alan Maley and Alan Duff

Games for Language Learning
by Andrew Wright, David Betteridge and Michael Buckby

Discussions that Work – Task-centred fluency practice *by Penny Ur*

Once Upon a Time – Using stories in the language classroom
by John Morgan and Mario Rinvolucri

Teaching Listening Comprehension *by Penny Ur*

Keep Talking – Communicative fluency activities for language teaching
by Friederike Klippel

Working with Words – A guide to teaching and learning vocabulary
by Ruth Gairns and Stuart Redman

Learner English – A teacher's guide to interference and other problems
edited by Michael Swan and Bernard Smith

Testing Spoken Language – A handbook of oral testing techniques
by Nic Underhill

Literature in the Language Classroom – A resource book of ideas and activities *by Joanne Collie and Stephen Slater*

Dictation – New methods, new possibilities
by Paul Davis and Mario Rinvolucri

Grammar Practice Activities – A practical guide for teachers
by Penny Ur

Testing for Language Teachers *by Arthur Hughes*

The Inward Ear – Poetry in the language classroom
by Alan Maley and Alan Duff

Pictures for Language Learning *by Andrew Wright*

Five-Minute Activities – A resource book of short activities
by Penny Ur and Andrew Wright

Five-Minute Activities

A resource book of short activities

Penny Ur
Andrew Wright

with illustrations by Andrew Wright

CAMBRIDGE
UNIVERSITY PRESS

Published by the Press Syndicate of the University of Cambridge
The Pitt Building, Trumpington Street, Cambridge, CB2 1RP
40 West 20th Street, New York, NY 10011–4211, USA
10 Stamford Road, Oakleigh, Melbourne 3166, Australia

© Cambridge University Press 1992

First published 1992
Sixth printing 1994

Printed in Great Britain by Bell & Bain Ltd, Glasgow

Library of Congress Cataloging-in-Publication Data

Ur, Penny.
Five-minute activities : a resource book of short activities /
Penny Ur and Andrew Wright.
p.   cm. – (Cambridge handbooks for language teachers)
Includes bibliographical references (p.).
ISBN 0-521-39479-1. – ISBN 0-521-39781-2 (pbk.)
1. Language arts (Elementary) 2. Activity programs in education.
I. Wright, Andrew, 1937– . II. Title. III. Title: 5-minute
activities. IV. Series.
LB1576.U7 1991
372.6–dc20   91–13302

British Library cataloguing in publication data

Ur, Penny
   Five-minute activities: a resource book of short activities.
   1. English language
   I. Title II. Wright, Andrew
   428

ISBN 0 521 39479 1 hardback
ISBN 0 521 39781 2 paperback

WD

Contents

The activities

Thanks

We would like to thank Michael Swan and Alison Silver for their editorial guidance, support and care.

The authors and publishers are grateful to Oxford University Press for permission to reprint the chant 'Sh! Sh! Baby's sleeping' on p. 43, from *Jazz Chants* by Carolyn Graham, copyright 1978 by Oxford University Press.

Introduction

This book provides a collection of short, easily-prepared activities to supplement the longer teaching procedures that make up the main body of an English course.

The need for short activities

When preparing your lesson, you start by planning the main items you want to include: the teaching of a new grammar point, for example, or a grammar exercise, or the reading of a text. But once you have prepared the main components of your lesson, and made sure it is (hopefully!) learning-rich, varied and interesting, you may find you still need some extra ingredients to make it into a smooth, integrated unit. You may need, for example:

1. a quick warm-up for the beginning to get your students into the right mood for learning;
2. an idea for a brief vocabulary review before starting a new text;
3. a light filler to provide relief after a period of intense effort and concentration;
4. a brief orientation activity to prepare a change of mood or topic;
5. a game or amusing item to round off the lesson with a smile.

Besides contributing to routine lesson planning, you may find these activities can be of use in non-routine situations as well: when, for example, you have to fill in for another teacher and need some quick, easily-prepared ideas for instant use; or for supplying extra content for an English club evening or English party; for helping a group of new students to get to know one another; or for keeping students profitably busy when you unexpectedly have extra time on your hands.

The activities

The process of each activity is described briefly, with examples; in many cases sample material for immediate use is provided in the BOXES.

Learning value

We have included only teaching procedures which we consider to have genuine learning value for the students. We have thus left out activities which we feel to be mere timefillers, or that keep students occupied doing something relatively profitless. (For example, we have not included the game 'Hangman' which has the class spending several minutes over the spelling of a single word!) We feel strongly that even in brief, enjoyable 'transition' activities the students can and should continue to practise, learn, increase knowledge and improve thinking.

Level

In most cases, activities are suitable for a variety of levels, from elementary to advanced, so you will find indication of a recommended level only in very few cases. You, the teacher, are probably the best judge of the appropriacy of an activity for your students. To give extra flexibility of level, you will find that the sample material in the BOXES is often clearly divided into elementary, intermediate and advanced sections.

Timing

As the title of this book implies, the activities are designed to be completed in about five minutes of lesson time, but some can be even shorter and others can be lengthened. We have in many cases added further ideas (under the subtitle *Variations*), which will enable you, should you wish, to develop the activity into a longer lesson component. Note that the first time a class uses a particular technique it might take a little longer than subsequent times, because of the extra minutes taken up with instructions and clarifications.

Preparation

Another guideline we have tried to observe is that the activities should demand the minimum of preparation before the lesson. Usually all you have to do is leaf through the book and decide which idea you want to use: the book itself provides the texts where necessary. Occasionally the activity demands a little planning before the lesson: where, for example, magazine pictures or small picture cards are needed. For the most part, the only materials are blackboard, chalk (or whiteboard, markers), and – for the students – their current textbook, pencils and notebooks or sheets of rough paper.

Integrating the activities into the lesson

The fact that the activity is short means that it is necessary to devote some thought to its introduction and ending, otherwise the frequent changes cause a feeling of abruptness and restlessness. Try to link each short activity with what has gone before or what is coming after, in topic, mood or language, by saying, for example: 'In that exercise, we came across two words that sounded the same but had different meanings. Let's look at some others . . . ' (see, for example, **Same word, different meanings**, page 68) or: 'We're going to be reading a poem about a journey, so let's start thinking about the idea of travelling . . . ' (see **Brainstorm round a word**, page 4). Even if you are using the activity as a total contrast, or as a rest or break with no connection with other parts of the lesson, it is worth making your reasons explicit: 'You all look as if you need a bit of a rest. Sit back and relax, I'm going to tell you a story and I'm NOT going to set you any questions on it!' Then, of course, make a link with the same sort of transition comment at the end: 'I hope you enjoyed that story and are feeling more relaxed. Right, now let's get back to . . . '

In order to explain the organisation of an activity, you will usually have to give an example of what is to be done. However, once the activity is clear, it is advantageous if the students or a student can take over the teacher's role. For example, there is no reason why a student should not ask the questions in **General knowledge** on page 30. As this principle applies to most of the activities it has not usually been referred to in the *Procedure* sections.

Organisation

The activities are laid out simply in alphabetical order of title. You may find it helpful to leaf through and note down for yourself names of activities you think you may want to use; you will then easily find them when you need them.

If, however, you are not looking for a particular title, but want an activity which practises *spelling*, or which stresses *listening* comprehension, or which involves the use of *guessing* or *mime* or *dictation*, you may find what you need by using the **Index** at the back of the book.

We hope you enjoy using this book as much as we have enjoyed writing it!

The activities

Abstract picture

Describing and vocabulary practice.

Procedure: Draw a big rectangle on the board. Draw in the rectangle a variety of squiggles, doodles, shapes (and colours if you have them). Ask the class what they think the picture represents. Assure the students that there is no right or wrong answer and encourage them to use their imaginations.

Adjectives and nouns

Position of adjective before noun; vocabulary.

Procedure: Students suggest adjective–noun phrases, for example, 'a black cat', 'an expert doctor'. Contribute some yourself. As the phrases are suggested, write the adjectives in a column down the left-hand side of the board, and the nouns on the right-hand side, so you will get something like this: ⇛→

a black	cat
an expert	doctor
a brilliant	student
a tidy	room
a rainy	day
a difficult	problem

Then they volunteer ideas for different combinations, for example 'a black doctor', and you draw a line to join the two words. See how many the class can make. If someone suggests an unusual or strange combination, they have to justify it – can you justify 'an expert cat', for example?

Variation: For an advanced class you might try adverb–adjective combinations: 'desperately miserable', 'reasonably fair', etc.

Amazing facts

Listening.

Procedure: You and your students may like the idea of having a regular five-minute slot in your lesson called 'Amazing facts'. In this session you or a student have five minutes in which to inform the class about something they may not be familiar with and which is likely to amaze them. An obvious source of information is the *Guinness Book of Records*, available in most countries and brought up to date every year. Books of statistical information from government sources or from specialist institutions are another source.

Instead of trying to fill a five-minute slot, a single amazing statement can be made. It might well provoke some discussion. Here is a brief example: 'People often say that it is always raining in Britain, but the annual rainfall in London is only 61 cm. In Brussels it is 72 cm, in Lisbon it is 68 cm, in Milan it is 94 cm, and in Geneva it is 86 cm.'

Ambiguous picture

Describing and vocabulary practice.

Procedure: Draw a small part of a picture. Ask the students what it is going to be. Encourage different opinions. Do not confirm or reject their ideas. Add a little more to the drawing and ask the question again. Build your picture up in about four stages.

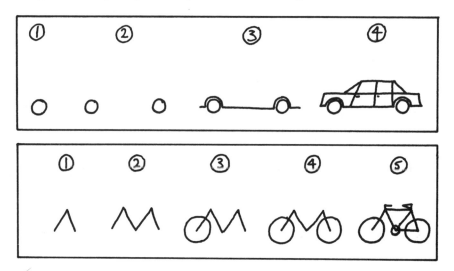

Associations

Vocabulary review and enrichment through imaginative association.

Procedure: Start by suggesting an evocative word: 'storm', for example. A student says what the word suggests to him or her – it might be 'dark'. The next student suggests an association with the word 'dark', and so on round the class.

Other words you might start with: sea, fire, tired, holiday, morning, English, family, home, angry. Or use an item of vocabulary the class has recently learnt.

Variation: If there is time, after you have completed a chain of about 15–25 associations, take the final word suggested, write it on the board, and, together with the class, try to reconstruct the entire chain back to the original idea.

Blackboard bingo

Listening, reading and vocabulary revision.

Procedure: Write on the board 10 to 15 words which you would like to review. Tell the students to choose any five of them and write them down.

Read out the words, one by one and in any order. If the students have written down one of the words you call out they cross it off. When they have crossed off all their five words they tell you, by shouting 'Bingo'. Keep a record of what you say in order to be able to check that the students really have heard all their words.

Variation: The procedure above demands recognition of sound and spelling relationships. You can make the activity more demanding by giving, for example, a definition of the words. The students must then listen for meaning and match this definition with their words.

Note: If, at the end of the lesson, there are a number of sentences or individual words written on the board you can use them for **Blackboard bingo**.

Brainstorm round a word

Vocabulary review and enrichment.

Procedure: Take a word the class has recently learnt, and ask the students to suggest all the words they associate with it. Write each suggestion on the board with a line joining it to the original word, in a circle, so that you get a 'sunray' effect. If the original word was 'decision', for example, you might get:

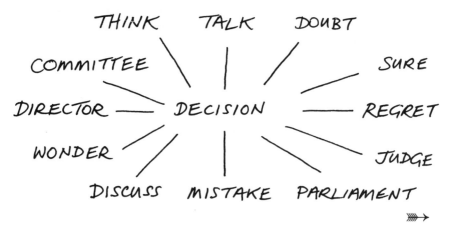

»»→

Or, at a simpler level:

The same activity can, of course, be done as individual or pairwork instead of in the full class.

Note: The same activity can be used as an introduction to literature. Take a central theme or concept of a story or poem you are planning to read with the class, and brainstorm associations in order to open and direct students' thinking towards the ideas that they will encounter in the text.

Variation 1: Instead of inviting free association, limit it in some way. For example, invite only adjectives that can apply to the central noun, so 'decision' might get words like: free, final, acceptable, wrong, right; and 'clothes' ones like: black, old, smart, warm, beautiful. Or invite verbs that can apply to the noun, for example: you can take, make, agree with, cancel or confirm a decision; and you can wear, tear, wash, buy, throw away or keep your clothes.

Variation 2: A central adjective can be associated with nouns, for example, 'warm' could be linked with: day, food, hand, personality. Or a verb can be associated with adverbs, for example, 'speak' can lead to: angrily, softly, clearly, convincingly, sadly.

Variation 3: For more advanced classes a word root can be used as the starting point, such as 'part' (leading to words like: partition, depart, partake, participate, impart). Alternatively, use prefixes (be–, de–, e/ex–, in/im–, inter–, per–, pro–, sub–, syn/sym–, trans–, etc.), or suffixes (–ant/ent, –able/ible, –ful, –ous, –ment, –ness, –tion, etc.).

Variation 4: As a follow-up, erase everything on the board, except for the central word. Challenge your class to recall and write down as many of the brainstormed words as they can.

Categories

Listening comprehension of isolated words.

Procedure: Ask the students to draw two or three columns on paper, and give them a category heading for each. For example, food and drink, or animal, vegetable, mineral. Then dictate a series of words which can fit into one of the categories. They have to write a cross or tick in the appropriate column for each word you dictate. For example, the headings 'Food' and 'Drink', and the items 'tea, apple, bread, coffee, cake, water, egg, meat' might result in:

FOOD	DRINK
✗	✗
✗	✗
✗	✗
✗	
✗	

For ready-to-use examples, see the BOX.

Note that you will need to note down the crosses yourself as you dictate the words in order to check the results.

Variation: For a more difficult and time-consuming exercise, students actually write out each word in its appropriate column. This will result in something like:

FOOD	DRINK
apple	tea
bread	coffee
cake	water
egg	
meat	

»→

BOX: Categories

Elementary

Food, drink: tea, apple, bread, coffee, cake, water, egg, meat, beer, milk, chocolate, potato, rice, pasta, orange juice.

Animals, objects: dog, pencil, chair, elephant, door, man, lion, book, table, cat, horse, donkey, television.

Big, small: elephant, mouse, matchbox, house, flower, mountain, pencil, cigarette, egg, sea.

Round, square: sun, book, blackboard, ball, window, door, moon, television, flower, house, ring, wheel, desk.

Land, sea, air: cloud, earth, rain, fish, tree, wave, fog, sky, field, ship, road, mountain, wind, swimmer.

More advanced

Sad, happy: smile, tears, laugh, miserable, tragedy, cheerful, pleasure, depressing, fortunate, celebration, weep, amusing, mourn, joke, delight.

Loud, soft: shout, scream, whisper, crash, murmur, rustle, roar, hum, bang, sigh, squeak, cheer, thunder, tick.

Good, bad: ethical, evil, wicked, virtuous, immoral, naughty, villainous, faulty, saintly, perfect, excellent, deplorable.

Superior, inferior: servant, queen, master, chief, subordinate, commander, assistant, slave, captain, prince, follower, head.

Sick, healthy: well, fever, fit, energetic, disease, pain, flourishing, sickness, invalid, blooming, collapse, coma, fine.

Chain story

Narration: use of the past tense.

Procedure: Begin telling a story. This can be the first few lines of a story from your coursebook, or improvised, or you can invite a student to start. Then, going round the class, each student has to add another brief 'instalment' to the story.

Variation: Before you start, ask each student to choose a word. It can be an item of vocabulary recently learnt, a verb in the past tense, or freely chosen. Then each 'instalment' has to include the word the student has chosen.

Changing sentences

Practice of sentence patterns.

Procedure: Choose a simple sentence pattern, which can be based on a grammatical structure you have recently learnt. For example, if you have been studying indirect objects, take a sentence like:

She wrote a letter to her sister.

Then students invent variations, either by changing one element at a time:

She wrote a letter to her husband.

Or by changing as much as they like, provided they maintain the original pattern:

The pilot sent a signal to the airport.

See how many variations they can make in two or three minutes.

Variations: Some coursebooks have pattern tables to guide students in the composition of correct sentences. These look something like this:

We People Children Dogs	often never sometimes always usually	eat sit on play with	the floor. meat. chairs. dolls. chocolate. balloons.

In the coursebook, students are usually expected to make sensible sentences like:

Children sometimes play with dolls.

For a quick, entertaining variation, tell the students to make ridiculous combinations:

Dogs often sit on chocolate.

Or, more seriously, to substitute elements of their own to make true sentences:

I never eat meat.

8

Compare yourselves

Getting to know each other; use of comparatives.

Procedure: In pairs, students find different ways of comparing themselves with each other, and write down or simply say the appropriate sentences.

> You are taller than I am.
> Tina has longer hair than I have.
> Jaime is older than Luiz.

Variation: To encourage more interaction, tell the students they may not use aspects (such as height or hair colour) that are immediately apparent, but only things they have to find out through talking:

> Peter has more brothers than I have.
> Marie knows more languages than Diane.

As a follow-up, share some of the things participants have found out with the rest of the class.

Comparing things

Practice of comparatives, *both*; opposites.

Procedure: Present the class with two different (preferably concrete) nouns, such as: an elephant and a pencil; the Prime Minister and a flower; a car and a person (preferably using vocabulary the class has recently learnt). Students suggest ways of comparing them. Usually it is best to define in what way you want them to compare, for example, by using comparatives:

> A pencil is thinner than an elephant.

Or by finding differences:

> The Prime Minister is noisy and a flower is silent.

Or similarities:

> Both a car and a person need fuel to keep them going.

Variations: You can give a whole set of related nouns together, for example, names of different foods, animals, household objects, or well-known people. Then each student can choose which two of them they wish to compare in each response.

If you have a little more time, start by eliciting a set of such items from the students, and writing them up at random on the board. As each student suggests a comparison, link the two items with a line. Then you can go back later and see if participants can remember what sentence is represented by each line.

Controversial statements

Discussion of controversial topics.

Procedure: Write up two or three controversial statements, or proverbs, on the board (there are some examples in the BOX). Each student writes down 'agree' or 'disagree' or 'don't know' for each item. Invite them to compare their answers in pairs or threes.

   Then find out what the majority opinion on each is, by vote. If you have time, discuss them.

BOX: Controversial statements

1. Beauty is only a matter of taste.
2. Riches are for spending.
3. Punishment never does any good.
4. A foreign language can only be learned, not taught.
5. A woman's place is in the home.
6. Boys and girls should have the same education.
7. A country gets the government it deserves.
8. Teaching is basically a matter of explaining things properly.
9. Married people are happier than unmarried people.
10. Love means never saying you're sorry.
11. People work better if they are paid more.
12. Everyone is basically selfish.

Correcting mistakes

Identifying and correcting mistakes in English, to encourage monitoring by students of their own mistakes.

Procedure: Write up a few sentences on the board that have deliberate mistakes in them. If you wish, tell the students in advance how many mistakes there are in each sentence. With their help, correct them. There are some examples of possible sentences in the BOX, in order of difficulty, together with the corrected versions. Or, better, use (anonymous!) examples taken from their own written work.

Note: It is important to stress the fact that the sentences initially presented are unacceptable, and to make corrections on the board so that the students are left with the image of the correct sentences at the end of the activity. $\ggg\!\!\to$

BOX: Correcting mistakes

Elementary

1. He love her very much.
2. They maked a cake for thier mother.
3. Wich one you prefer?
4. I not know were to go.
5. This one is gooder then that one.
6. Were is the girl go?
7. Why you look at me like that?
8. You must to tell my!
9. The flowers was in the garden.
10. Yesterday I am very ill.

More advanced

1. She asked me where am I going.
2. I am living here since six years.
3. I would have came if you asked me.
4. The mony was stole by a theif.
5. Where is the boy which you were looking at him?
6. He looked me after for much time.
7. She raised slowly the hand.
8. They will come, isn't it?
9. When I am younger, I was used to go to school.
10. You need the courage to do such thing.

Corrected versions (elementary)

1. He loves her very much.
2. They made a cake for their mother.
3. Which one do you prefer?
4. I don't / do not know where to go.
5. This one is better than that one.
6. Where is the girl going?
7. Why do you look / are you looking at me like that?
8. You must tell me!
9. The flowers were in the garden.
10. Yesterday I was very ill.

⟫→

11

Were is the girl go?

Crosswords

Vocabulary review.

Procedure: Ask a student to write a word of not more than five letters in the middle of the board, for example, 'melon'. The letters should be written clearly and separately.

Now you should think of a word which shares one letter with the word on the board. Give the students a clue to your word. For example, 'I like reading them.' If somebody guesses 'books', he or she writes the word so that it crosses the first word and shares a letter. The students now take over from you. Ask for a student to think of a word running horizontally using one letter from the word 'books' or vertically sharing a letter with 'melon'. That student should give the class a clue for the word, its length and its first letter. Continue building up the crossword alternating between horizontal and vertical words. See how many words the class can think of in five minutes.

⟫→

```
      b
      o
m e l o n
      k
      s
```

Variation 1: Draw a grid of 100 squares. Proceed as above with students thinking of words and giving the clues.

Variation 2: If you wish to follow up this work on another occasion, ask the students to write down the clues for each word in the puzzle. You can then give the puzzle to another class to solve.

Variation 3: If you have a small class, this activity can be used as a way of introducing and learning names. Begin with one student's name and see if the other students can write their own names on the board sharing at least one letter with those already written.

Cutting down texts

Forming new grammatical sentences by eliminating words or phrases from the original.

Procedure: Take a short text of up to about 30 words (it can be from your coursebook), and write it up on the board. Students suggest any section of one, two or three words that can be cut out, while still leaving a grammatically acceptable – though possibly ridiculous – text. Sections are eliminated for as long as it is possible to do so.
    For example:

The princess was awakened by the kiss of a handsome prince.

The princess was awakened by the kiss of a prince.

The princess was awakened by a prince.

The princess was awakened.

The princess!

Princess!

Variation: The students then try to reconstruct the original text.

Acknowledgement: Based on an idea in *Once Upon a Time* by John Morgan and Mario Rinvolucri (Cambridge University Press, 1983).

Damaged property

Guessing; using the past tense and passives.

Procedure: Present a brief description of a piece of property that is damaged: a watch that has stopped, for example, or a suitcase with the handle missing. You need to have in your mind the reason for the damage; the students try to guess what it is. Allow 'narrowing-down' questions ('Did it happen because of carelessness?') and give hints ('It happened while I was cooking . . . ') to maintain pace and ensure the students' ultimate success in guessing. The successful guesser can suggest the next damaged item.

It is best if the items can be genuine, with genuine histories – yours or the students'. Or use the examples in the BOX.

Acknowledgement: Based on an idea in *Grammar in Action* by Christine Frank and Mario Rinvolucri (Pergamon, 1983).

BOX: Damaged property

1. A watch that has stopped (dropped into the soup while I was cooking).
2. A suitcase with the handle missing (a thief tried to steal it, I pulled it back, he got away with the handle).
3. An umbrella with a hole in it (someone's lighted cigarette fell on it).
4. A pencil with the lead broken off (I tried to open my desk drawer with it).
5. A book with some pages torn out (took it camping and urgently needed paper to light a fire).
6. Jeans that are torn and faded (done on purpose to be more fashionable).
7. A car that won't start (battery run down because the lights were left on all night).
8. A squashed cake at a picnic (the youngest member of the family sat on it).
9. A hole in the roof (a small meteor fell through it).
10. A broken window (a tree fell onto it during a storm).

>>>→

Delphic dictionary

Reading and discussing.

Preparation: You need at least one copy of an English–English dictionary for this activity.

Procedure: Ask the class to list on the board, from their own experience, some typical student problems. For example:

- having enough money
- relating to a 'difficult' person in the family
- deciding what to do in the future
- managing to do all the college work and have a good social life

Show the dictionary to the class and ask a student to help you. They must put the dictionary on a desk, close their eyes, let the dictionary fall open at any page, spin their forefinger around in the air and then let it fall randomly on the open page of the dictionary. They should then read out the word and its definition to the class. Ask the class to suggest how the word and definition could be the basis of advice for a student who has the first problem.

For example, 'having enough money':

A student lets the dictionary fall open, spins her finger round and drops it on 'macaroni'. She reads out, 'Italian *pasta* (= food made from flour mixed with water) in the shape of thin pipes, cooked in boiling water.' Another student says, 'She's so poor that she must eat macaroni every day.' Another student says, 'She works in an Italian restaurant in the evenings to make some money.' ⟫→

Variation 1: If there are enough dictionaries in the classroom, let the students work in groups or pairs, first noting down their problems and then giving and discussing advice.

Variation 2: Use a dictionary of proverbs or a dictionary of idioms. Less effective but possible, ask the students to use any list of language items, for example, in their student books.

Note: You might like to tell the students about the oracle at Delphi in Greece. In Delphi there is a very old Greek temple, built around 2,500 years ago, which was very famous because the people in the temple, the priestesses, gave advice. People came from all over Greece to get advice from the priestesses. However, the advice was never clear. One king went for advice: he didn't know whether he should begin a war or not. The priestesses told him that if he went to war a great kingdom would be lost. He thought, 'Good, I will go to war and win!' He went to war and lost his own kingdom!

For more on the use of dictionaries in this way, see *How to Improve Your Mind* by Andrew Wright (Cambridge University Press, 1987).

Detectives

Practice of affirmative, negative and question forms of the past.

Procedure: One volunteer is the detective and goes outside. You give a coin to one of the students in the class to hide on their person – he or she is the thief. The detective returns and accuses any member of the class: 'Did you take the money?' The accused, whether guilty or innocent, answers, 'No, I didn't take the money, X (names one of the others) took it.' The detective then accuses X, using the same formula as before, and so on, until ten or fifteen people have been accused (it is up to the students to make sure that the real thief is named). The detective watches the accused people and has to try to 'detect' by their behaviour which one is lying. Give him or her three 'guesses'.

Variations: Use 'Do you have / Have you got?' instead of 'Did you take?' Alternatively, imagine the 'criminal' did other 'crimes' in order to practise other verbs: broke a window, stole a book, ate someone's lunch, etc.

Diaries

Writing.

Procedure: Ask the students to keep a diary, and allow five minutes once or twice a week for this to be done. The diary can be about the students' experience of the lessons and what they feel they have achieved, or it can be about other matters of concern to them.

The diary does not need to follow the convention of a day-by-day record. It can be kept private, or shared with another student and/or shared with you. Note that this is not an appropriate vehicle for correcting mistakes of language.

Dictate numbers

Grasping the meaning of numbers quickly and translating into figures.

Procedure: Dictate a random list of numbers in English. Both you and the students write down the corresponding figures as you say them. Then check, by writing the answers on the board, or asking them to reformulate their figures into words.

Variation: Ask the students to add up the numbers you dictate – do they get the right result?

Discussing lessons

Discussion.

Procedure: Five minutes before the end of a lesson ask the students how the lesson was divided and what basic activities were done. Write these on the board. Indicating one of the activities, ask what the students feel they got from it. You might ask if they felt it could have been improved as an activity. Ask if the learning point needs more work in future lessons. When a point has been made by one student, check with the class as a whole to find if the view is shared.

You might conclude by summarising what you were trying to achieve and what you feel you have learned from their feedback.

Variation 1: Ask the students to write their experience in the form of a letter addressed to you. Try to reply to each student if you possibly can.

≫→

Variation 2: Ask the students to appraise a longer period of time than a single lesson. Design a chart for them to complete. An example is given in the BOX.

BOX: Discussing lessons

ENGLISH LESSONS ASSESSMENT

Give a mark out of ten for each:

silent reading	
talking activities	
listening activities	
writing essays	
textbook exercises in class	
grammar explanations	
general organisation	
homework	
English lessons generally	

Add other things you think are important

Comments

What the teacher might do to make the lessons better

What I might do to make the lessons better

Don't say yes or no

Oral questions (mainly yes/no) and short answers.

Procedure: One volunteer student stands in front of the class. The rest fire questions at him or her, with the aim of eliciting the answer 'yes' or 'no'. The volunteer has to try to answer the questions truthfully without these words. This will mostly be through the use of 'tag' answers such as 'I did' or 'She does not'. If the volunteer does say the forbidden words, he or she is 'out' and another is chosen. Give a time limit of one minute; if within that time the volunteer has not said 'yes' or 'no', he or she has won.

Variation: The class is divided into two teams. A student from team A answers questions from team B, until he or she says 'yes' or 'no'. Then it is the turn of someone from team B to answer team A. Time each turn carefully. The winning team is the one whose representative has lasted longer without pronouncing the forbidden words!

Draw a word

Vocabulary review.

Procedure: Whisper to one student, or write down on a slip of paper, a word or phrase that the class has recently learnt. The student draws a representation of it on the board: this can be a drawing, a symbol, or a hint clarified through mime. The rest of the class has to guess the item.

Variation: This technique can also be used to guess proverbs, once the class has learnt a number of them (see **Proverbs** on page 63).

English words in our language

Study of cognates or loan words from English in the students' mother tongue.

Procedure: In pairs or small groups the students think of as many words as they can in two minutes that they know were originally English but are commonly used in their own language. Write up all the words on the board. Alternatively, do the activity as a competition and see which group has the most words.

Obviously, this activity is easier to do if members of the class share the same mother tongue, but it can still be done in multi-lingual classes: groups are challenged to find English-origin words that are used in all, or most of, their languages.

Note: This is a good morale booster for beginners or false beginners: it demonstrates to them how many English words they in fact know, even without advanced knowledge of the English language itself.

Erasing words

Spelling.

Procedure: Write on the board about ten words which are difficult to spell, and give the class a minute to 'photograph' them. Point to one word, then erase it; the students write it down from memory. And so on, until all the words have been erased. Check the spellings.

Evidence

Information-gap discussion; use of the 'logical necessity' modals *can* and *must*.

Procedure: Two students stand with their backs to the board: they are the 'detectives'. You write up a brief situation (for examples, see the BOX). The rest of the class are 'witnesses' and suggest, orally, concrete evidence (sounds, sights, smells, etc.) for the existence of the situation, without mentioning the situation itself; the 'detectives' have to deduce it from the evidence.

For example, if the situation is 'The school must be on fire', the 'witnesses' might say:

⟫→

I can smell smoke.
It's getting hotter in here.
I can hear the alarm bell.
People are jumping out of the window.

Variation: If you have more time, the activity can be organised as a team game, with each team taking it in turns to provide 'detectives' and be 'witnesses'.

BOX: Evidence

1. She must love reading.
2. The lesson must be boring.
3. They can't like me very much.
4. That child must be ill.
5. He can't have studied for the test.
6. Someone must be at the door.
7. She must have run all the way here.
8. That car must have been in an accident.
9. It must be time to go home.
10. It can't be very cold outside.
11. You must have a cold.
12. He must have hurt his foot.
13. She must be from the USA.
14. He can't be in a very good mood.
15. My house must have been burgled.
16. There must be a party at that house.
17. That girl must be very popular.
18. That child must be lost.
19. It must be a public holiday.
20. He can't have washed for some time.
21. That woman must be very rich.

Expanding headlines

Building grammatical sentences; current affairs.

Procedure: From an English-language newspaper pick out an abbreviated headline, like 'OIL SPILL OFF WEST COAST', and write it on the board, or just read it out. The students write out the information in full sentence form, for example: 'A quantity of oil has been spilt into the sea off the west coast.'

Variation: Students expand the headline as much as they can, adding extra information they happen to know about the news item in question – names, times, causes, results, etc. – but keeping within the one-sentence limit. Who has the longest, most informative sentence?

Expanding texts

Forming grammatical sentences by adding words or phrases.

Procedure: Write a single simple verb in the centre of the board. Invite students to add one, two or three words to it. For example, if the word was 'go', they might suggest 'I go', or 'Go to bed!' They go on suggesting additions of a maximum of three consecutive words each time, making a longer and longer text, until you, or they, have had enough.

The rule is that they can only add at the beginning or end of what is already written – otherwise you will end up with a rather untidy (and hard to read) series of additions. Add or change punctuation each time as appropriate. For example:

Go
Go to bed!
"Go to bed!" said my mother.
"Go to bed!" said my mother angrily.
"You must go to bed!" said my mother angrily.
"You must go to bed!" said my mother angrily.
"No!" I answered.
...etc!

⟫→

22

Variation: Students can erase the additions in reverse order, starting with the last addition and ending with the original word in the centre of the board.

Acknowledgement: Based on an idea in *Dictation: New methods, new possibilities* by Paul Davis and Mario Rinvolucri (Cambridge University Press, 1988).

Express your view

Speaking and listening.

Procedure: Near the beginning of term, tell the students that you want each of them to be ready to talk for exactly four minutes on a subject they care about.

Each week select a name randomly (perhaps from names in a hat). That student must prepare his or her talk for the following week. At the end of the talk the other students can ask questions and express how they feel about the ideas expressed.

Guidance to the student:
1. The talk should take into account the short time available, who the other students are and the circumstances of the room in which the talk is to be given.

  It is a good idea for the student to try out the talk beforehand and make sure it does not exceed four minutes. This leaves one minute for one or two other students to respond.
2. Pictures, objects and tapes can be used to support the talk but not to substitute it.
3. Examples of topics:
   - a description of an interesting experience
   - a description of a hobby
   - an explanation of a technique for doing something
   - an expression of pleasure in an experience
   - an expression of belief
   - an argument for change
   - the presentation of a dilemma
   - persuasion for the other students to take a particular course of action
   - any topic which the student feels confident about and which can be presented in a very short time

Fact and fiction

All the skills.

Procedure: Ask all the students to write a statement which is either true or false. Choose ten students at random to take it in turns to read out their sentences. The rest of the class (including the nine students who are actually reading out their own sentences) note down their names, listen carefully and make a tick or cross according to whether or not they think each student's sentence is true or false. When the ten students have finished, compare responses and then ask the ten students to say whether their sentences were true or false.

Note: The students should make statements about facts which can be proved, for example, annual rainfall in a particular place or the broadcast that evening on television of a particular film. Too many unfounded assertions lead to a breakdown of the activity.

If the reference source is in the classroom, there can be no dispute. For example, you might like to ask the students to make true or false statements about a picture they can all see or a text they have just read.

Family tree

Listening comprehension and brief writing.

Procedure: Make sure the students know what a family-tree diagram is. You may have to explain and illustrate.

Describe a family. The students draw and write the corresponding family-tree diagram as you do so. For example, the description: 'Tom and Mary are married, and they have two children. The elder is Rose and the younger is Tim' would lead to the following simple family tree:

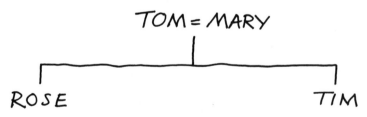

Remember this is virtually a dictation, so make sure students have time to think and write. Then sketch the family tree on the board so they can check their results. ⟫→

Family trees can be improvised, or, better, use a family you know personally (your own?), or one that features in a popular television programme, or one well known in the country (such as the Royal Family in Britain).

Variation: After the class has done this once from your description, students can try dictating their own family trees to each other.

Favourites

Brief reading and discussion; survey of class tastes.

Procedure: Write on the board about five or six names of items or topics in the same field: television programmes, for instance, or foods, colours, songs, singers, politicians, school subjects, etc. Identify each by a letter: A, B, C, etc. For example, you might give:

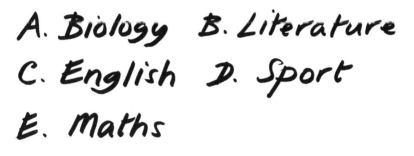

A. *Biology*   B. *Literature*
C. *English*   D. *Sport*
E. *Maths*

Each student writes down the letters in order of preference: if sport is the favourite then the student will write D at the top of the list. Those who finish early can compare and discuss their choices with their neighbours. When they have all finished, hold a vote to see which choices were most popular. If you have time, discuss different tastes, and see if there is a general consensus on favourites.

Favourite words

Vocabulary review.

Procedure: Write on the board one of your favourite words. Tell the class it is one of your favourite words and explain why. It can be a favourite for any reason you like: it sounds nice to you; it looks nice; it's so useful; it reminds you of good friends, occasions, places, etc. If you feel the students need more examples of words and reasons for liking them, write one or two more on the board.   ⟫→

The students should now write down some of their favourite words and then give their reasons for choosing them to their neighbour. Some students might volunteer to write their favourite words on the board and give their reasons for liking them to the class.

Variation: Talk about words you don't like.

Acknowledgement: Encouraging students to develop a personal and subjective association with the foreign language is now widely accepted as rewarding for them. Many activities towards this end are to be found in *Vocabulary* by John Morgan and Mario Rinvolucri (Oxford University Press, 1986).

Feel the object

Vocabulary review.

Procedure: Collect various objects from the students and from around the room. You can do this by asking the students to bring them to you. Put the objects in a bag. Hold the bag and then ask students to feel the objects and to try to identify them.

Finding the page

Quick dictionary search (provided all the class have the same dictionary).

Procedure: Write up or dictate a series of words (possibly ones they have learnt recently). The students have to find each word in the dictionary and write down the number of the page where it appears. You, of course, have to do the same! How many of the words can they find the right pages for in three, four or five minutes?

Note: The aim of the exercise – which the students should be made aware of – is to improve their speed and efficiency in finding words in the dictionary.

Variation: For monolingual classes that have standard bilingual dictionaries, give a word in the native language. They then have to find the page where the English equivalent appears – but at the English end of the dictionary. For instance, if you give a class of French students the word 'rouge', they have to look up and find the English word 'red'.

Find someone who

Brief pair conversations.

Procedure: The students have one minute to walk around the room and find at least one person in the class who was born in the same month as they were: they get one point for every person they find in the time. Then they have to find someone who was born on the same day of the month. Give further similar tasks for as much time as you have (see the BOX for suggestions). At the end, see how many points each student has.

BOX: Find someone who

Find someone who . . .

  was born in the same month as you.

  was born on the same day of the month as you.

  has the same number of brothers as you.

  has the same number of sisters as you.

  ate at least two of the same things as you for breakfast.

  has the same favourite colour as you.

  got up at the same time as you did this morning.

First, second, third

Vocabulary review.

Procedure: Ask about ten students to stand up at the front of the class. Ask them to arrange themselves in the alphabetical order of their first names. When they are in order they should each say their name. (If you wish, they could also say the names of all the other students in the line.)

The students who are still in their seats can take part by commenting on the correctness of what the students at the front are doing and saying.

Variations: The same students or another group can continue this type of ordering activity in the following ways:
- Standing in order of their birthdays through the year (if this is culturally important for the students). They should then give their birthday dates in turn.
- Standing in the alphabetical order of their family names, the regions they come from, or the towns or villages they come from.
- Standing in the order of the distance they come to school / the class.
- Standing in the order of the times at which they get up or go to bed.

Five-minute writing storms

Writing.

Procedure: Tell the students that they have exactly five minutes to write about something. Set a subject which you feel will focus the students' minds but encourage personal rather than generalised responses (see the BOX).

Tell them that you will not mark any mistakes of language but will only be concerned with the ideas or experiences they describe. (You can note down general errors and give a language focus activity on these forms at another time.)

For the next lesson, prepare general comments and select texts written by the students, to read out.

Variation: The students write for exactly three minutes and then take it in turns to read what they have written to each other.

⤷

```
┌─────────────────────────────────────────────────────┐
│  BOX: Five-minute writing storms                    │
│                                                     │
│  Themes                                             │
│  The best thing in the lesson today                 │
│  The worst thing in the lesson today                │
│  The best thing to happen to me today               │
│  Something which is not fair                         │
│  A jealous moment                                   │
│  A generous act                                     │
│  A sad (frightening/funny/strange/great) moment     │
│  What is friendship?                                │
│  A road                                             │
│  A door                                             │
│  A dilemma                                          │
│  A memory from my childhood                         │
│  A memory from my first school                      │
│  What is in my head at this moment?                 │
│  A place I know                                     │
│  A person I know                                    │
│  Something I hate (or love) doing                   │
│  My favourite TV programme                          │
│  My favourite possession                            │
│  An unexpected meeting                              │
└─────────────────────────────────────────────────────┘
```

Flashing

Describing and vocabulary review.

Preparation: If you want to flash a magazine picture, you will need to mount it on card.

Procedure: You can flash any of the following for a brief moment: a picture mounted on card or in a book; a text on a strip of card; a book cover; a newspaper headline; an object. The students then identify and/or describe what they saw. Encourage differences of opinion and do not confirm or reject any ideas. Flash several times to promote attempts at identification and discussion. In the end, show the text, picture or object.

⟫→

Note: Pictures and texts on transparency and solid objects can be flashed on the OHP. Do not turn the light on and off as this destroys the lamp: flick a book rapidly underneath the lens instead. Choose pictures or texts which are reasonably clear.

General knowledge

Discussion.

Procedure: Announce a general knowledge quiz and then ask the kind of questions given in the BOX opposite. The students can volunteer answers or you can ask them to write down what they think the answer might be.

Variation 1: Ask each student to research and write down at least three questions and answers. Ask them to give their reference for their facts. Use these in the quiz.

Variation 2: Divide the class into groups of four. Ask the questions and give the students exactly 45 seconds to discuss each question and to agree on an answer in their groups. Each group gives its answer and then you (or a student in the role of quiz master) give the authoritative answer. ⟫→

BOX: General knowledge

Elementary level

1. Where is Mount Everest?   (Nepal/Tibet border)
2. How high is Mount Everest?   (8,848 metres)
3. Where do anteaters live?   (South America)
4. What is the capital city of Uruguay?   (Montevideo)
5. Where does the two-humped camel live?   (The two-humped Bactrian camel lives in the Central Asian Steppes.)
6. What are the differences between African and Indian elephants?   (The African elephant has larger ears and longer back legs.)
7. Where is the Eiffel Tower? Which country and which city?   (France/Paris)
8. What is the official language of Chile?   (Spanish)
9. What are the colours of the French flag?   (Red, white and blue)
10. What colour do you add to blue in order to make purple?   (Red)
11. Which is the longest river in the world?   (The Amazon and the Nile are about the same length.)
12. How long is the longest river in the world?   (6,448 km for the Amazon and 6,670 for the Nile. However, it is impossible to be absolutely sure.)
13. Which is the highest waterfall in the world?   (Salto Angel in Venezuela – 979 metres)
14. Which is the biggest country: the United Kingdom, France or Spain? (The UK: 240,937 km^2; France: 547,026 km^2; Spain: 504,782 km^2)
15. Which river flows through London?   (The Thames)
16. What and where is the Valley of the Kings?   (A place where many kings and people of the court were buried – in Luxor, Egypt.)
17. What is SOS in the international Morse code?   ($\cdots ---\cdots$)
18. What is the American English word for the *boot* of a car?   (Trunk)
19. Where is the Sea of Tranquillity?   (The moon)
20. What are the shortest words in English?   (*a* and *I*).

Intermediate level

1. Who invented the aeroplane?   (The first powered flight was by Wilbur Wright in 1903. It lasted 12 seconds.)
2. Who is the Queen of the United Kingdom?   (Queen Elizabeth II)
3. Who was the most famous woman Prime Minister in Britain?   (Margaret Thatcher, 1979–90)
4. Who invented gunpowder?   (Gunpowder was probably invented in China in about 1160.)

⟫→

5. Which is the most famous long island?   (Long Island in New York State, containing Brooklyn, Queens and John F. Kennedy Airport)

6. What did John Boyd Dunlop invent in 1888?   (He made tyres with air in them for his child's bicycle.)

7. Who wrote *King Lear, Macbeth* and *Romeo and Juliet*?   (William Shakespeare)

8. What do English-speaking people often say when they are being photographed?   ('Cheese!' Then they look as though they are smiling.)

9. If it is midday in London, what time is it in New York?   (Seven o'clock in the morning)

10. Which was the most expensive film ever made?   (*Star Trek* in 1979: $46,000,000)

11. Which of the Beatles was killed?   (John Lennon)

12. Why was Leonardo da Vinci famous?   (He was an outstanding thinker, painter, architect and inventor in Italy, 1452–1519.)

13. What is the boiling point of water?   (100° centigrade)

14. Name at least three countries in Europe which have red, white and blue flags.   (United Kingdom, Czechoslovakia, France, Luxembourg, Netherlands, Norway)

15. Which river flows through Cairo?   (The Nile)

16. What are the first six letters on the top row of most typewriters in the world?   (QWERTY)

17. What does UNESCO stand for?   (United Nations Educational, Scientific and Cultural Organisation)

18. Which is the nearest big city to Heathrow Airport?   (London)

19. What is the American English word for the British English word *lift*? (Elevator)

20. Which is the bigger, the American billion or the British billion?   (The British billion. American billion = one thousand million. British billion = one million million; this is called a 'trillion' in American English.)

Advanced level

1. Is it possible to go by ship to Paraguay?   (No, Paraguay has no sea coast.)

2. Can you give at least two meanings of *park*?   (a) an enclosed piece of land for recreation;   b) to position and leave a vehicle)

3. If you were in Freetown in South Africa in August, would you be wet or dry?   (Wet. The rainfall is very heavy in August, averaging about 80 cm.)

4. Which three nationalities did Einstein have at different times?   (He was born in Germany, then became a Swiss citizen, and later took American citizenship.)

5. Which metal boils at the highest temperature: silver, gold or lead? (Gold: 2,900°C; silver: 2,210°C; lead: 1,740°C)

⟫→

6. Which President died a violent death in 1963? (John F. Kennedy)
7. When did Elizabeth II become Queen of the United Kingdom: 1948, 1952, 1965 or 1974? (1952)
8. What happened if you killed a cat in ancient Egypt? (You were executed because cats were sacred.)
9. What is the symbol of the zodiacal sign Taurus? (Bull)
10. Which French woman beat the English? (Jeanne d'Arc or Joan of Arc won several battles against the English in the 15th century before she was captured and burned to death.)
11. Which Roman town was covered by volcanic ash? (Both Pompeii and Herculaneum were covered by ash from Mount Vesuvius in 79 AD.)
12. What is the last event in the decathlon? (1,500 metres)
13. How is the year 1500 written in Roman numerals? (MD)
14. Which letter begins the least number of words in English? (x)
15. Who was the Iron Lady? (Margaret Thatcher, Prime Minister of the United Kingdom from 1979–90)
16. Who was the Queen of Egypt twice? (Cleopatra, 51–48 BC and 47–30 BC. Her brother was king for one year, then Julius Caesar helped Cleopatra to get her throne back again.)
17. Who arrived in Australia before Captain Cook? (The Aborigines were there 20,000 years before the Europeans. The first Europeans were the Portuguese in the 16th century.)
18. Which island was first seen from a Dutch ship on Easter Day in 1772? (Easter Island)
19. Which are the winter months in the Southern Hemisphere? (June to August)
20. Who was the close friend and assistant of Sherlock Holmes? (Dr Watson)

Acknowledgement: Chief sources for the information in these questions: *The Guinness Book of Records* (1986 edition) and the *Macmillan Encyclopedia* (revised edition 1983).

Getting to know someone

Sharing information and getting to know other students.

Procedure: Ask the students to list three or four things they like to know about people they have just met. Working in pairs, each student then chooses one of the areas in the other student's list and asks them questions about it.

≫→

Variation: Working in groups, the students can pool the things they like to know about other people. They then take it in turns to choose an area of interest and to ask the others questions about it.

Guessing

Yes/no questions and answers.

Procedure: Choose an object, animal or person, and tell the students which of these categories it belongs to. They have to guess what it is. Encourage 'narrowing-down' questions, and give generous hints if the guessing slows down or seems not to be progressing towards the right answer. The student who guesses the answer chooses the next thing to be guessed.

Variations: Instead of defining the item to be guessed by saying whether it is an object, animal or person, give different hints: whether it is animal, vegetable or mineral; the first letter of the word ('I spy with my little eye something beginning with . . . '); the colour; the size, whether you like it or not, etc.

The number of questions can be limited to 10 or 20.

Hearing mistakes

Listening comprehension with quick reactions.

Procedure: Tell or read a story that is well known to the students (it can be one they have recently worked on in class), introducing deliberate mistakes as you do so. When they hear a mistake, students put their hands up, call out the correction, or note down the mistake.

How do you feel?

Describing feelings.

Procedure: Tell the students to close their eyes; they might like to place their heads on their arms. Ask them to think about how they feel; they might think about their day so far, or about their previous lesson with you and what they remember of it, what they learnt and what their problems might have been. After a few minutes, students who are willing to do so can say what their feelings are.

Acknowledgement: How to Be a Peaceful Teacher by J. Wingate (Pilgrims Publications and The Friendly Press, 1987).

How many things can you think of that . . . ?

Vocabulary revision.

Procedure: In groups, students try to think of and note down as many things as they can that fit a given definition and that they know in English. For instance, you might tell them to think of as many items as they can that are small enough to fit into a matchbox. After two or three minutes, pool all the ideas on the board, or have a competition to see which group can think of the most items. See the BOX for more ideas for definitions.

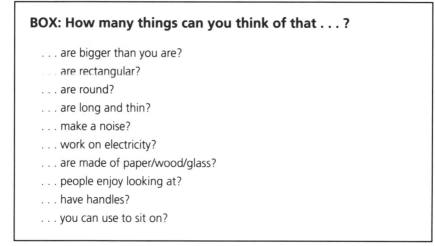

BOX: How many things can you think of that . . . ?

. . . are bigger than you are?

. . . are rectangular?

. . . are round?

. . . are long and thin?

. . . make a noise?

. . . work on electricity?

. . . are made of paper/wood/glass?

. . . people enjoy looking at?

. . . have handles?

. . . you can use to sit on?

If I had a million dollars

Practice of conditionals; imaginative situations.

Procedure: Tell the students to imagine that a million dollars (or an equally large sum in the local currency) is to be won by the person who can think of the most original (or worthwhile, or exciting) thing to do with the money. Listen to their ideas and decide who has 'won'.

If I weren't here

Conditionals; sharing ideas.

Procedure: The students note down the answer to the question: 'If you weren't here, where would you be?' Share ideas. Then introduce a slight variation: 'If you weren't here, where would you *like* to be?'

Other similar questions: 'If you weren't yourself, who would you like to be?' Or: 'If you weren't living now, when would you have liked to live?'

Imaginary classroom

Describing a room; use of prepositions.

Procedure: Tell the students to imagine that the room is absolutely empty: no furniture, no people, nothing. They have to create their ideal classroom by suggesting how to 'refurnish' it. For example:

There is a thick soft wall-to-wall carpet on the floor.
There is a television in that corner, with a video.

Imaginative descriptions

Descriptions.

Preparation: Any two pictures large enough for the class to see clearly.

Procedure: Hold up two pictures chosen at random and ask the students to suggest a possible relationship between them. Encourage imaginative, even ridiculous ideas. For example, a picture of a car and a picture of a packet of cigarettes:

>>>→

Student A: They are both dangerous to other people, not only to the driver or to the smoker.

Student B: They both give a lot of taxes to the government.

Student C: The driver of that car wants to stop smoking so that he can pay for the car.

Student D: I don't like it when people smoke in a car.

Note: The connections can be personal, or they can be more objective and part of other people's experience, as in the examples above.

Variations: You can ask the students to imagine a connection between any two items: picture/picture; text/text; picture/text. The texts can be short or long, written or spoken.

Imaginative identifications

Imaginative identification and vocabulary practice.

Procedure: Hold up a pen and start a conversation.

You: What's this?

Student: A pen.

You: No, it isn't! (*Pretend to fly the pen around as if it were a plane.*) What is it?

Student: It's a plane.

Give the pen to a student and ask him or her to pretend that it is something else. Continue around the class for as long as imaginative ideas are forthcoming.

If the students need more inspiration, you might like to make use of a few examples from the BOX.

Acknowledgement: We first saw Alan Duff demonstrate this idea.

⫸→

BOX: Imaginative identifications

Objects and what they could represent:

Pen: plane/telescope/screwdriver/nail/boat/flute/mouth organ/etc.

Exercise book: roof/bird/telescope/table tennis bat/mirror/etc.

Chair: horse/car/person/garden fork/washbasin/animal/etc.

Bulldog paper clip: footballer/bird/scissors/etc.

Cup: hat/microphone/bird's nest/face and nose/hammer/etc.

Bag: washbasin/hat/balloon/book/monster's mouth/etc.

Important people

Discussion.

Procedure: In small groups or pairs, students tell their neighbours which person (or people) has been an important influence in their lives and why.

I'm pulling your leg

Listening.

Procedure: Tell the students about a real experience or plan of yours, but mix in some fantasy elements. Here is an example, based on a plan to spend the evening playing chess with an old friend. Keeping a straight face, but with a twinkle in the eye, say:

> 'Oh, I am looking forward to this evening! You won't believe me! I don't think I have told you before but I play chess. I am so famous that chess players from all over the world come to play against me. Haven't I told you? Yes, I know it's difficult for you to believe. But this evening Boris Karpov, the Russian grand master is coming. Of course, it will be a difficult match . . . '

By this time (if not before!) your students will be expressing their disbelief. Admit that you may have exaggerated a little and ask them which parts of the story they think are true.

Variation: Divide the class into groups of four or five. The students then take it in turns to tell a story which is either true with fantasy elements added, or wholly true, though difficult to believe, or wholly untrue. The other students listen and say which elements, if any, are true.

Interrupting the story

Listening and asking questions.

Procedure: Tell the students that you are going to begin a story and that they should try to stop you saying more than a few words by asking questions. For example:

> *You:* The other day . . .
> *Student A:* Which day was it?
> *You:* It was Tuesday.
> *Student B:* Was it in the morning or afternoon?
> *You:* Afternoon. Anyway, I was . . .
> *Student C:* What time was it?   etc.

Acknowledgement: We first experienced this technique with Alun Rees in Barcelona.

Interview an interesting personality

Asking questions; interviewing.

Procedure: Imagine that you are a person who is well known to the students: a famous national figure, a singer or actor, a local personality, or a character from a book. You are at a press conference; the students are the journalists. Tell the students who you are and invite them to ask you questions; you, of course, have to improvise answers, as convincingly as you can. After the first time, a student can take over the role of the 'interviewee', choosing his or her own new identity.

It is helpful to allow the students a minute or two to jot down ideas for questions before starting the 'interview'.

Variation 1: Instead of taking on a new identity, be yourself, but with some interesting fact about yourself for the students to ask questions about. This can be genuine: an interesting hobby, experience, or personal situation. Or it can be imaginary: you have a pet elephant, or have just returned from a year alone on a desert island, or are going to spend an evening with someone famous. The students ask you questions about the interesting fact you have mentioned. The answers often generate further questions, and an interesting semi-serious interview develops.

Variation 2: The person to be interviewed (you or a volunteer student) tells the class he or she is a well-known personality, but does not tell them who. They ask questions in order to find out the person's identity. Once they have discovered it, the interview continues as described above.

Invention technique: modifying

Discussion; conditionals.

Procedure: Tell the class that you have learned a technique for helping them to be inventive and to think of new ideas. Say that you will demonstrate one of these techniques. Write words for two objects on the board, for example:

ball   **book**

Ask the class to help you to list the characteristics of one of the objects. For example:

ball round; sometimes bounces; different colours; sometimes floats; water does not spoil it; does not get broken

Now ask the class to suggest any advantages in designing the second object like the first one, for example, designing a book like a ball:

- it would bounce and would not be damaged if it were dropped
- if the book were boring you could bounce it and play a game with it
- if it were a forbidden book people wouldn't know because they would think it was a ball
- if it were a ball it wouldn't matter if it got wet
- if the words were all over a ball you could turn it in any direction and invent your own story

Now ask the class if these would be serious advantages and if they could really be applied in some way to books.

Invention technique: reversing

Discussion.

Procedure: Write the name of a manufactured product on the board, for example, a book. Ask the students to list the characteristics of a book. For example:

- it has words in it which tell you something
- it has pages
- it is made of paper

                                                ⟫→

- it is printed
- you can buy it in a bookshop

Now ask the students to try to imagine complete opposites of all the characteristics of the object. For example:

- it has no words in it, only pictures/symbols/numbers
- it doesn't have pages
- it's solid / a continuous sheet / a film
- it isn't made of paper, it's made of steel/rubber/plastic/air
- it isn't printed, it's empty
- you can't buy it in a bookshop, it's free / you can buy it in a supermarket

Ask the students if they can design a new object by choosing some of these 'opposite' ideas and seeing if any of them could make sense. For example:

- It could look like a book but it could be empty like a box. You could hide things in it.
- It could look like a book but it could be a computer.
- It could look like a book but it could be a sandwich box.
- It could look like a book but be solid. Supermarkets could give them away and you could put a lot of them on your shelves and people would think you were intelligent.
- It could look like a book but be a television. Children would buy them and their parents and teachers would think they were reading when really they would be watching television programmes.

For more creative techniques, see *How to Improve Your Mind* by Andrew Wright (Cambridge University Press, 1987).

Invisible elephant

Vocabulary review.

Procedure: Tell the students that you are going to draw a picture for them. Draw the outline of an elephant in the air with your finger. Ask them what you have drawn. Encourage different interpretations.

Note: Draw the elephant as a continuous line rather than 'sketching' it in the air and going from one side to another, indicating details in the middle of the shape, wrinkles in the skin, etc.

It was the way she said it

Intonation, stress and rhythm.

Procedure: Take one word or a short sentence and ask the students to say it in as many different ways as possible. You might like to discuss with the students what difference the intonation makes to the meaning in each case, or in what circumstances this intonation might be used. See the examples in the BOX.

BOX: It was the way she said it

1. I love you
2. Oh
3. Hello
4. Good morning
5. Well
6. Come here
7. Please
8. You
9. Yes
10. No

I would like to be a giraffe

Discussion.

Procedure: Write down the following words on the board:

lake waterfall river ocean

Each student decides which of these he or she would prefer to be and tells his or her neighbour. They ask each other follow-up questions, for example: 'Is it a very high waterfall?' 'Is it a lake in the mountains or a lake in flat country?' 'How do you think an ocean shows your personality and interests?'

See the BOX for further ideas.

⋙→

```
┌─────────────────────────────────────────────┐
│                                             │
│  BOX: I would like to be a giraffe          │
│                                             │
│   giraffe/dog/cat/lion                      │
│   sun/moon/star/comet                       │
│   glass/bowl/box/cup                        │
│   Rome/New York/London/Paris                │
│   path/motorway/lane/road                   │
│   chair/bed/bath/cupboard                   │
│   hat/sock/jacket/scarf                     │
│   orange/green/brown/purple                 │
│   cabbage/orange/banana/potato              │
│   tree/flower/grass/vegetable               │
│   head/toe/leg/arm                          │
│                                             │
└─────────────────────────────────────────────┘
```

Acknowledgement: We first came across this idea in the work of Mario Rinvolucri.

Jazz chants

Listening and singing.

Preparation: Write the chant below on a transparency, a large sheet of paper, or on handouts.

Procedure: Demonstrate the chant by reading it with slightly emphasised but natural speech rhythms. After one reading ask the class to repeat, in chorus, the refrain 'What did you say?' When you feel the students are confident and enjoying it, divide them into two groups. Ask one group to read the verses and the other to read the refrain.

I said, Sh! Sh! Baby's sleeping!
I said, Sh! Sh! Baby's sleeping!

What did you say?
What did you say?

I said, Hush! Hush! Baby's sleeping!
I said, Hush! Hush! Baby's sleeping!

What did you say?
What did you say?

I said, Please be quiet, Baby's sleeping!
I said, Please be quiet, Baby's sleeping!

What did you say?
What did you say?

⟫→

I said, Shut up! Shut up! Baby's sleeping!
I said, Shut up! Shut up! Baby's sleeping!
WAAAAAAAAAAAAAAAAAAAAAA!!!
Not anymore.

Variation: When the students are familiar with the idea of a jazz chant, ask them to try writing their own.

For more chants, see the following books and cassettes:

Jazz Chants for Children by Carolyn Graham (Oxford University Press, 1979)
Jazz Chants by Carolyn Graham (Oxford University Press, 1978)
Small Talk by Carolyn Graham (Oxford University Press, 1986)

Jumbled sentences

Forming grammatical sentences.

Procedure: Pick a sentence out of your coursebook, and write it up on the board with the words in jumbled order:

early the I week to during have to go sleep

The students work out and write down the original sentence:

I have to go to sleep early during the week.   *or*
During the week I have to go to sleep early.

If there is time, give a series of similar sentences, and the students do as much as they can in the time.
You can use this activity to review a grammatical point, taking the sentences from a grammar exercise.

Variation: Dictate the jumbled sentences instead of writing them up; the students write them down as you dictate and then suggest the solutions orally.

Jumbled words

Vocabulary and spelling practice.

Procedure: Write on the board words the students have recently learnt, or ones they have difficulty spelling (see the BOX on pp. 79–80) with the letters in jumbled order. It is best to have the words all associated with one given theme, otherwise the task of working them out can be too difficult and time-consuming.

For example, you might give an elementary class a set of words like:

gdo, sumoe, owc, knymoe, tca, tnhpeeal, ibdr

and tell them these are all animals. In the time given they work out as many as they can of the answers:

dog, mouse, cow, monkey, cat, elephant, bird.

Kim's game

Vocabulary review.

Procedure: Say that you are interested in seeing how observant the students are and what sort of memories they have. Collect about seven or eight objects belonging to the students (with their agreement!). Let the class see each object before you put it into a bag. If there is sufficient time, ask the students to write down from memory the names of all the objects, what they look like and who they belong to. If time is short, ask the students to call out the names of the objects, their appearance and who they belong to. (You can check these by looking in the bag.) Do not immediately confirm or reject descriptions. Encourage argument! Finally, show the objects and return them to their owners.

Likes and dislikes

Discussion.

Procedure: Ask each student to write down three things they like and three things they don't like. They can decide whether they wish to refer to important things or to less important things, but what they write must be true.

Do the same thing yourself. Read out a point from your list and then add some information to it. For example? 'I don't like loud noise, particularly if it's unnecessary. If it's necessary I can put up with it', etc.

»»→

Encourage the students to ask you questions. Students then contribute their likes or dislikes.

Variation: Working with their neighbours, students take it in turns to read out their points to each other and to chat further about them.

Listening to sounds

Vocabulary and past tense forms.

Procedure: The students close their eyes and rest their heads on their arms. They should then listen and try to recognise all the sounds they hear. If some students deliberately contribute to the noises to be identified, that is useful, but don't let it get out of hand!

After two minutes they open their eyes and describe and discuss what they heard, first with their neighbour and then with the class as a whole.

Note: Both the simple past tense and continuous past tense are naturally contextualised by this activity. Example:

There was a car; it was going past. It was accelerating. Somebody dropped something. I think it was a lot of wood . . . or some bricks. Somebody was whispering in the class. Somebody was laughing. Somebody closed a door. There was a bird; it was singing.

Magical entertainment

Reviewing tense forms.

Preparation: You need a postcard (or a similar size of card or paper) and a pair of scissors.

Procedure: Choose the biggest student in the class. Say you are going to cut a hole in the postcard, then ask whether he or she could climb through it. Get each student in the class to commit him or herself to a prediction.

Cut the card as follows:

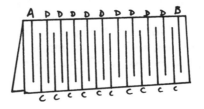

⟫→

Step 1. Fold the card in half, lengthways.
Step 2. Make two cuts, A and B.
Step 3. Cut along the fold from A to B.
Step 4. Now do alternate cuts C, D, C, D, etc., cutting through both halves of the folded card.
Step 5. Shake out the zigzag circle of card and ask the student to climb through it.

Having cut the card, show it to the class and ask if they think that the student will be able to climb through it.

If you wish, use the following tense forms:

– going to cut / climb through the card
– cutting / climbing through the card
– has cut / climbed through the card

Note: Your trick may stimulate a whole succession of tricks done by the students. Other sources of magic tricks include: *Games for Language Learning* by Andrew Wright, David Betteridge and Michael Buckby (Cambridge University Press, 1984); *How to Be Entertaining* by Andrew Wright (Cambridge University Press, 1987); *English by Magic* by Peter Hassel (Pergamon Press, 1985).

Making groups

Vocabulary review.

Procedure: Decide what lexical area you wish to review. Ask the students to call out all the words they know related to that area. Two student 'secretaries' should write the words on the board as the class call them out. Ask the students to think of as many different ways of grouping the words as possible. If you have coloured chalks (or pens if you have a whiteboard), ask the secretaries to encircle the various words they feel belong to one kind of grouping.

car lorry/truck wheel engine accident
seat fast *traffic lights* driver petrol/gas
speed sign road motorway/highway police
bus garage taxi bicycle key oil

Note: As an alternative to the use of chalks, the words can be written quickly with felt pen on strips of paper which are then fixed to the board. The strips can then be moved around to form different groups.

Variation: Ask pairs of students to write down the words in groups and then tell you what groups they have found. They should be able to say what each group is based on, for example, 'All these words are to do with motor vehicles.'

Martian

Describing.

Procedure: Draw a picture of a Martian on the board.

Place your two forefingers on either side of your head and tell the class that you are a Martian. Pretend that you are unfamiliar with everyday objects, for example, cars, coffee, ships, music. Pretend also that you do not have a very wide vocabulary in English. The students should try to help you to understand what each object or idea is, but you must continually ask questions as if you don't understand. For example:

    Martian: What's a car?
    Student A: People travel in cars.
    Martian: What is 'travel in'?
    Student B: 'Travel' means you go from one place to another place.
    Martian: But what does a car look like?
    Student C: It's like a box on wheels.
    Martian: What's a box?   etc.

Match the adjectives

Vocabulary review.

Procedure: Write three adjectives on the board. For example:

important dangerous heavy

Ask the students to suggest things which could be described by all three adjectives. For example:

Student A: A car.
Student B: A plane.
Student C: An army.
Student D: A printing machine.

Variation: In pairs, ask the students to jot down three adjectives and as many things as they can think of which those adjectives could describe. Take three adjectives chosen by one pair of students, write them on the board and ask the class to suggest things which the words might describe. Compare and discuss the pair's suggestions with those of the class.

Acknowledgement: This activity is based on 'Word profiles' in *Vocabulary* by John Morgan and Mario Rinvolucri (Oxford University Press, 1986).

BOX: Match the adjectives

beautiful/big/cold
green/young/expensive
small/lucky/free
small/loud/fat
expensive/wonderful/hot
expensive/heavy/interesting
wonderful/exciting/dangerous
tall/thin/thirsty
fast/favourite/expensive
funny/small/thin

Match the people

Vocabulary review.

Procedure: Write a list of about ten jobs on the board. Each student writes down a list of ten ideas, feelings, memories, etc. he or she associates with one of the jobs listed. (The name of the job referred to must not be included.) For example, here is a list of associations with a job given in the first line of the BOX:

> poor, expensive, colour, canvas, pain, joy, brush, smell, country, friends.

Each idea must be described by a single word. The students then work in pairs, and each student studies his or her neighbour's list and tries to guess which job the list refers to. The student then confirms or rejects the guess and explains why he or she put each word in the list; the connection may not always be obvious. For example:

> *Artist:* the words without an obvious connection are, perhaps, 'smell' (smell of the oil paint), 'country' (painting in the country), 'friends' (friends who are artists).

BOX: Match the people

actor/actress/architect/artist/baker/businessperson/butcher/chemist/clerk/
cook/dancer/dentist/doctor/driver/factory worker/farmer/footballer/grocer/
policeman/policewoman/postman/postwoman/seaman/secretary/singer/
teacher/vet/waiter/waitress/writer

Memorising words

Memorising new words.

Procedure: Divide the board into two halves. Write in one half vocabulary which the students have only just encountered and which you would like them to remember. Ask the class to pick one of the new words and to suggest a word they know which it reminds them of in some way. Write this 'reminding word' on the other side of the board. Having written the 'reminding word', erase the new word. Do this with each of the new words until they have all been replaced by 'reminding words'. Now ask the students what each 'reminding word' was linked to. Write in the new words again and erase the 'reminding words'.

>>>→

Acknowledgement: This activity is closely modelled on one described by Richard and Marjorie Baudains in their book *Alternatives* (Longman, 1990).

Metaphors

Imaginative comparison; discussion.

Procedure: Discuss with the class the concepts of 'simile' and 'metaphor'. What metaphors can they find for a teacher, and why? For example: a teacher is a parent – he or she encourages and cares about the progress or his or her charges; a teacher is the compere of a variety show – he or she introduces, ends and comments on activities.

Give the students a subject and a series of possible metaphorical comparisons (see the BOX); ask them individually to choose which they think most appropriate and why. Then they compare and talk about their suggestions with partners or in a class discussion.

Variation: Once the students have grasped the idea, give only a subject, and ask them to find their own metaphors for it.

BOX: Metaphors

1. **A teacher:** a film director, a book, a counsellor, a policeman/woman, a car, a manager, a signpost, an artist, a key, a walking stick.
2. **A lesson:** a variety show, a telephone conversation, a wedding, a mountain climb, a menu, a game of football, a song, painting a picture.
3. **A student:** a flower, an artist, a climber, a hunter, a puppet, a lump of clay, a soldier, a philosopher.
4. **A family:** a house, an octopus, a fire, a garden, a bed, a hand, a river, a chain.
5. **Beginning school/this course:** opening a door, jumping into cold water, turning on a light, planting a seed, setting out on a journey, signing a contract, joining a club, sitting down to a meal.

Miming

Vocabulary review.

Procedure: Write a list of vocabulary on the board which you feel should be reviewed. Students take it in turns to mime one of the words so that the class can identify the word that he or she has chosen.

≫→

Note: Words for physical actions lend themselves to mime. However, it is also possible to mime jobs, feelings, objects, qualities of objects, proverbs and even abstract concepts.

It helps the students to mime and to identify each other's miming if there are a limited number of words listed on the board. Ask the students to jot down the word they are going to mime on a piece of paper and give it to you before they begin!

Variation 1: Divide the class into two teams. Let students from each team take it in turns to choose a word from the board (student book, etc.) and mime it so that their own team can identify the word they are miming. The team which has identified the most words is the winner.

Variation 2: Ask a student to mime a series of related actions, for example, getting an egg from the fridge and boiling it. The other students must try to identify the actions and remember them in the right order. This variation makes natural use of the simple past tense form. You can ask the students to write down the actions they have identified before they call them out.

Miming adverbs

Manner adverbs; imperatives.

Procedure: One student goes outside, and the others choose a manner adverb (for example, 'quickly' or 'angrily'). The student returns and orders one of the members of the class to do an action by saying, for example, 'Stand up!' or 'Write your name on the board!' or 'Open the door!' The person addressed has to carry out the command according to the manner adverb chosen: to stand up quickly, or write their name angrily, for example. The student has to guess what the manner adverb was.

There are more examples of adverbs in the BOX.

BOX: Miming adverbs

Elementary adverbs: quickly, slowly, angrily, sadly, happily, quietly, loudly, lightly, heavily, strongly.

Intermediate adverbs: calmly, lazily, sleepily, fearfully, proudly, secretly, silently, painfully, lightly, seriously.

Advanced adverbs: dramatically, gracefully, decisively, apologetically, worriedly, thoughtfully, stiffly, jerkily, childishly, drunkenly.

Mistakes in reading

Listening.

Procedure: Select a text in the students' coursebook. Say that you are going to read the text aloud and they should follow in their own book. Add that you feel tired or haven't got your glasses and might make a mistake: they must tell you if you do. Read to the class, but substitute, add or omit words. The students should tell you immediately. Thank them, correct yourself and carry on making more mistakes.

Music

Writing and reading.

Preparation: You will need a tape recorder and a cassette of music you like and you think your students will like.

Procedure: Play the music. Ask the students to write what colour it reminds them of and why.
   Invite students to read their sentences to each other. Ask one or two students to read their sentences to the class as a whole.

Variation 1: Play the music. The students write what sort of person the music makes them think of.
   Invite the students to read their descriptions to each other.

Variation 2: Play the music. The students write what sort of scene they imagine.
   Invite the students to read their descriptions to each other.

Variation 3: Play the music. The students write the story they imagine.
   Invite the students to read their descriptions to each other.

Variation 4: Use the music as a non-verbal break when you feel the students would benefit from relaxation and will be able to concentrate better as a result.

Acknowledgement: All these ideas derive from an article written by David Cranmer in 'Practical English Teaching', September 1990, pages 33–4.

C

My neighbour's cat

Review of adjectives.

Procedure: Draw a cat on the board.

Introduce it as your neighbour's cat. Say, 'My neighbour's cat is an awful cat!' Write the word 'awful' on the board. Write all the letters of the alphabet under the *a* of awful. Say, 'What can you say about your neighbour's cat?' Tell the students that they can offer ideas in any order they like. As the ideas are suggested, write in the adjectives next to the appropriate letters.

> *You:* My neighbour's cat is an awful cat.
> *Student A:* My neighbour's cat is a wonderful cat.
> *Student B:* My neighbour's cat is a quiet cat.
> *Student C:* My neighbour's cat is a beautiful cat.   etc.

Note: Encourage the students to play with the adjectives; allow some 'poetic licence'. For example, we would not normally say 'guilty cat', but it is possible and it is amusing. If the students like the activity, you might use it to add new adjectives to their repertoire. Tell the students to use a dictionary.

You might like to jot down the words the class thought of and then continue the activity in another lesson.

⟫→

Variation 1: If you have time, ask the students to repeat what each person has said before, like this:

> *Student:* Mrs Bruno's neighbour's cat is an awful cat.
> Francesca's neighbour's cat is a wonderful cat.
> Berthold's neighbour's cat is a quiet cat.
> My neighbour's cat is a beautiful cat.

Variation 2: Ask the students to offer as many adjectives as they can think of which might refer to a cat, for each letter.

Variation 3: Write the name of a famous person below the cat. Ask for an adjective for each letter of the name, suitable for the famous person's cat.

Variation 4: Write down the name of someone in the class who has a cat (or any other kind of pet), for example, Richard. Ask other students for adjectives for each letter in the name. They should ask the owner of the pet whether their adjective is appropriate or not. They should then use a negative or an affirmative sentence.

> *Student A:* Richard, is your cat a daft cat?
> *Richard:* No, it isn't!
> *Student A:* Richard's cat isn't a daft cat.
> *Student B:* Richard, is your cat a charming cat?
> *Richard:* Yes, it is.
> *Student B:* Richard's cat is a charming cat.

BOX: My neighbour's cat

awful, amazing, angry, African, anxious, aggressive

bad, beautiful, big, black, blue, brown, bored, busy

cold, clever, cool, careful, careless, comfortable, cute

difficult, dirty, dark, dead, dear, different, daft

expensive, exciting, educated, excellent, extraordinary

famous, fat, funny, fast, favourite, fine, free, frightening, female

good, green, generous, greedy, guilty

happy, hot, hungry, hard, heavy, horrible

ill, important, interesting, impatient, innocent, intelligent

jealous, joyful, jolly

kind, kingly, knowledgeable

little, long, loud, large, lazy, light, lonely, lucky

mad, male, magic, mean, miserable, modest, musical, mysterious

nasty, new, nice, nervous, noisy ⟫→

---

old, obedient, official, ordinary, original

poor, painful, pale, patient, peculiar, perfect, pet, pink, polite, popular, powerful, proud

queer, quick, quiet

red, respectful, rich, round

sad, slow, small, short, soft, strong, secret, silent, special, strange, stupid, surprised, sweet, sick

tall, thin, thirsty, terrible, tiny, tough

unhappy, ugly, unconscious, unpleasant, unusual, unknown, untidy, unlucky, upset, useful

valuable, violent

white, warm, weak, wonderful, wild, wise

xenophobic (dislikes or fears strange or foreign people or customs)

young, yellow

zany (foolish in an amusing or absurd way)

Neighbours and neighbourhoods

Description.

Procedure: Divide the class into pairs. Give each student the letter A or B. Tell the A students to close their eyes and put their heads on their arms on the desk. Tell the A students that they should now try to describe their neighbour B's appearance to him or her from memory. B should help by asking questions and by commenting.

If there is time, reverse roles so that student B cannot see. Student B should then attempt to describe the front and back of the classroom; what is there and something about its appearance. Student A should respond but not confirm or reject B's description.

Variation 1: All the students try to remember what can be seen from the school/college front entrance. Encourage differences of opinion.

Variation 2: Agree on an experience which all the students have in common. This can be something of an everyday nature, for example, a school/college open evening or a fire safety practice in the college or even the first five minutes of the lesson. The challenge is, how well can the students remember things? They should attempt to reconstruct, in minute detail, the appearance and behaviour of the people involved and what they said, the sequence of events and the setting.

New comparisons

'As . . . as' comparisons.

Procedure: Teach the class a few 'as . . . as' similes commonly used, for example, 'as proud as a peacock' or 'as good as gold'. Then suggest a few adjectives, and ask them to invent their own comparisons. Share and discuss them.

See the BOX for further conventional similes and suggested adjectives for inventing new ones.

BOX: New comparisons

Conventional similes

as proud as a peacock

as good as gold

as warm as toast

as white as snow

as quick as lightning

as mad as a hatter

as sweet as honey

as cold as ice

as drunk as a lord

as light as a feather

as heavy as lead

Adjectives

Elementary: happy, long, short, beautiful, clever, clean, tall, small, rich, strong.

Intermediate: free, lazy, wise, powerful, innocent, ugly, smooth, faithful, fresh, colourful.

Advanced: juicy, graceful, brilliant, humble, irritable, sly, rotten, romantic, obstinate, delicious.

as mad as a hatter

New words

Learning/reviewing new vocabulary.

Procedure: Allow the students a minute or two to write one or more new words they have recently come across and think that other students may not know yet. Alternatively, they may use dictionaries to clarify the meaning of a new word picked out of a book. In pairs or small groups they then teach each other their words. If there is time, a group can share its new words with the entire class. Note down the words yourself for future review.

Numbers in my life

Guessing; giving personal information.

Procedure: Each student thinks of a number which is important in his or her life – a date, a telephone or house number, an age, or whatever. A volunteer writes his or her number on the board, and the others try to guess what it is and why it is important.

Odd one out

Vocabulary review.

Procedure: Write six words on the board from one broad lexical set. For example:

chair table window cupboard desk shelf

Ask the students which word does not 'belong' to the others. Challenge the students to argue why this word is the 'odd one out'. For example, a window is outside and inside a building and the other objects are all inside. Encourage students to argue that another word is the odd one out. One might say that chair is the odd one out because it is the only one that you normally sit on.

Variation: Each time you and the students agree that a word is the 'odd one out', erase it from the board until you are left with two words. Then ask the students to suggest ten ways in which these two words are different.

⟫→

Opposites

Vocabulary review and enrichment.

Procedure: Write on the board or dictate a series of six to ten words which have fairly clear opposites. In pairs or groups, the students help each other to think of and note down the opposites. Check, and supply any words the students did not know.

The BOX gives some suggestions for pairs of opposites. Note, however, that these are only suggestions, and for some items you or your students may wish to suggest other opposites that we have not thought of. In some cases, words may have two or more possible opposites, for example 'light': 'heavy' or 'dark'. Also, you should be open to original, imaginative suggestions from the students, provided these are accompanied by reasonable justification!

Variation: If by the end of the activity all the pairs of opposites have been written on the board, erase the original words you gave and see if the students can recall them from the ones remaining.

BOX: Opposites

Elementary

foot: head, hand	**cold:** hot
drink: eat	**far:** near
hard: soft, easy, gentle	**father:** mother, son

⟫➤

---

full: empty

boy: girl, man

old: new, young

fat: thin

short: long, tall

light: dark, heavy

buy: sell

summer: winter

clean: dirty

right: wrong, left

black: white

wife: husband

broad: narrow

arm: leg

begin: end

small: large, big

Intermediate

noisy: quiet, silent

accidentally: on purpose, deliberately

brave: cowardly

all: none

friend: enemy

ask: answer, reply

boring: interesting

bride: (bride)groom

cheap: expensive

remember: forget

increase: decrease, lessen

defence: attack

deep: shallow

lose: find, gain

polite: rude

together: apart, separate(ly)

maximum: minimum

punishment: reward

guilty: innocent

true: false

well: badly, ill, sick

cause: result

future: past

active: passive

stay: leave

asleep: awake

back: forward, front

die: live, be born

cool: warm

kind: unkind, cruel

war: peace

common: rare

simple: complicated, complex

fail: succeed

female: male

few: many

first: second, last

Advanced

single: double, married, multiple

admire: despise

concrete: abstract

hope: despair

rough: smooth, exact

amateur: professional

exterior: interior

vague: exact, precise

essential: optional

theory: practice

safety: danger, peril

holy: profane

poverty: riches

private: public

⟫→

extremist: moderate	**prosecution:** defence
coastal: inland	**raise:** lower
ascend: descend	**omit:** include
child: adult	**vacant:** occupied
bless: curse	**niece:** nephew, aunt
refuse: consent	**natural:** artificial
pride: humility, modesty	**native:** foreigner
contract: expand	**modern:** old-fashioned
conceited: modest	**ignorant:** educated, knowledgeable
absent: present	**drunk:** sober
accept: reject	**negative:** positive, affirmative
victory: defeat	**joy:** sorrow

Oral cloze

Listening comprehension.

Procedure: Read a story or prose passage, which can be from your coursebook. Stop occasionally before a key word and get the students to guess what it is going to be: they can either volunteer the word orally, or write it down. If the passage is one they have worked on recently, this can function as a review exercise of key vocabulary.

Picture dictation

Listening comprehension.

Procedure: Describe a scene or person, giving the students time to draw what you say. Let them compare pictures with each other. If there is time, they can then dictate the picture back to you while you draw it on the board.

Variation: This can be done the other way round: the students dictate a drawing to you, each contributing a different detail. Or they can work in pairs, dictating to each other.

Piling up a sentence

Present simple (or another tense); vocabulary review.

Procedure: Start by telling the students something you like, for example:

> I like pop music.

Then ask a student to recall what you like, and add a 'like' of his or her own:

> (The teacher) likes pop music, I like watching television.

Another student adds a further item:

> (The teacher) likes pop music, Jaime likes watching television, I like ice cream.

. . . and so on, with each student adding something, until the chain becomes too long to remember.

Variation: Instead of 'I like . . . ', the basic sentence might be 'I hate . . . ' or 'I want to buy . . . ' or 'Yesterday I . . . ', or 'When we are all millionaires, I will . . . ', or 'If we were given a single wish, I would . . . '. By choosing the appropriate basic sentence, this activity can be used to practise a tense or structure that has been learnt recently.

Prefixes and suffixes

(Advanced) vocabulary review and enrichment; awareness of English morphology.

Preparation: Choose a prefix/suffix you want to study and make for yourself a list of words that include it. For prefixes, the dictionary can be a useful source.

Procedure: Suggest a word prefix or suffix, and give the students a minute or two to write down all the words they know which begin or end with it. Then 'pool' all the words they have, write them on the board, and teach any extra ones you can think of. Note that in some cases the meaning of the prefix has an obvious connection with the meaning of the word (*sub* = under, *subterranean* = underground), whereas in others it does not (*subject*).

See the BOX for some suggested prefixes and suffixes to use.

Variation 1: If you have more time, give the students two or three different prefixes (or suffixes) simultaneously.

⟫→

Variation 2: As a follow-up, ask the students to invent their own new words using the prefixes or suffixes they have been working on (something, incidentally, which is constantly done naturally by native speakers), and to put them into sentences:

> I find this word quite unlearnable!
> This project needs a lot of pre-thinking!

BOX: Prefixes and suffixes

Prefixes

per- (through)	ante- (before)
pre- (before)	anti- (against)
re- (again, back)	auto- (self)
sub- (under)	co-, con-, com- (with)
super- (over, above)	circum- (around)
trans- (across)	dis- (not)
ab- (from)	e-, ex- (out of)
non- (not)	mis- (badly, wrongly)
inter- (between)	

Suffixes

-er, -or (agent, doer)	-able, -ible (able or deserving to be)
-ism (name of system, belief)	-ic (having the property)
-ist (name of believer in system)	-ify (to make __)
-ment (result of action)	-ise (bring into a specific state)

Proverbs

Learning and reviewing English proverbs.

Procedure: Write a well-known English proverb on the board (see the BOX for some examples). Discuss its meaning, and compare it with similar or contrasting proverbs from the students' own culture.

Variation 1: Compare proverbs that appear to contradict one another (2 and 3, for example in the BOX, or 9 and 10). Can the students think of circumstances or stories which might illustrate the truth of either proverb?

⟫→

Variation 2: From a list of ten or more proverbs, students choose which they would adopt as a personal motto, or suggest as a motto for the school/college/class.

BOX: Proverbs

1. It's no use crying over spilt milk.
2. Look before you leap.
3. He who hesitates is lost.
4. Still waters run deep.
5. Don't count your chickens before they're hatched.
6. Don't cross your bridges before you come to them.
7. Look before you leap.
8. First come, first served.
9. Absence makes the heart grow fonder.
10. Out of sight, out of mind.
11. Make hay while the sun shines.
12. Never say die.
13. Where there's a will there's a way.
14. There's no smoke without fire.
15. Better late than never.
16. Don't put the cart before the horse.
17. All that glitters is not gold.
18. You can't have your cake and eat it.
19. Experience is the best teacher.
20. Better safe than sorry.
21. When in Rome, do as the Romans do.
22. A bird in the hand is worth two in the bush.
23. No news is good news.
24. Live and let live.
25. Live and learn.
26. The more you have, the more you want.
27. Let sleeping dogs lie.

⟫→

A bird in the hand is worth two in the bush.

Questions about a statement

Practice in forming questions.

Procedure: Take a sentence which is a statement of fact – true, false, absurd, it doesn't matter – from your coursebook or from your own or the students' imagination. The students try to see how many questions they can ask about it. Example:

The moon is made of green cheese.

Possible questions:

Has the moon always been made of green cheese?
Is the cheese light or dark green?
Is the cheese hard or soft?
Is the moon all made of green cheese, or only part of it?
Why is the moon made of green cheese?
How was it made?
What does the cheese taste like?

... and so on.

Variation: If there is time, students try to think of answers to some or all of the questions.

Reasons for wanting an object

Discussion; imaginative argument.

Procedure: Tell the students you have an item to give away as a gift, and the person who can give the most convincing reason why he or she wants it will get it. The item can be something that is really desirable (a new car or a winter coat, for example); or something that is not (a baby crocodile or a stone) so that students really have to use their imaginations to devise reasons why it might be needed. See the BOX for suggestions; or use items you happen to have in your pocket or bag.

Variation: If you have a little more time, this can be done as a team game. For each item, each team should suggest as many reasons for needing it as it wishes, and you decide which is the most convincing. When you have run out of time, or the students have had enough, count up to see which team has won the most 'gifts'.

BOX: Reasons for wanting an object

Desirable objects

a car	a winter coat	an armchair
a radio	a stereo set	a television
a bicycle	a motor boat	a bottle of perfume
a gold watch	a box of chocolates	a bottle of wine

Not very desirable objects

an empty tin	a stone	a baby crocodile
a paper bag	a bit of string	a used envelope
a bone	an old newspaper	a single shoe
a feather	a bucket of mud	a playing card

Recalling words

Vocabulary review.

Procedure: Write on the board between 15 and 20 words the students have recently learnt, or that you think they know. Make sure all the words are understood. Give a minute for everyone to look at them, then erase or conceal them. Individually or in pairs or groups, the

⟫→

students try to recall as many as they can and write them down. Find out who remembered the most (and spelt them correctly).

Use an overhead projector for this activity, if you have one; then the words can be quickly and easily hidden and revealed.

Variation: Use whatever happens to be left over on the board after the previous activity as a basis for recalling.

Relaxation technique

Listening and relaxing.

Procedure: Tell the students to clear or at least to tidy their desks. Then tell them that you are going to help them to relax. If they have difficulty in accepting this proposal, you might point out that many athletes and professional performers use the technique you are going to demonstrate in order to relax.

In order not to interrupt the instructions you are going to give them, check that they are familiar with the words you are going to use, for example, 'rib cage'. You might judge that the students will concentrate better if they close their eyes. Say:

Sit up straight. Don't be stiff. Now, close your eyes, pull in your chin and imagine the top of your head reaching to the ceiling. Now I want you to breathe deeply. First of all, you should try to fill the lower part of your lungs. Place your hands flat and gently against the lower part of your rib cage. Your fingers should just touch. Breathe in slowly and naturally. When you breathe in, your abdomen should expand at the beginning of your breathing and your chest shouldn't move very much at this stage. Hold your breath, then let your muscles relax, and breathe out slowly and evenly. It is the breathing out which is so important for relaxation.

Now do it again.

Acknowledgement: How to Improve Your Mind by Andrew Wright (Cambridge University Press, 1987).

Rub out and replace

Changing text while maintaining grammatical accuracy.

Procedure: Write a sentence of about ten words on the board, which can be from the coursebook.

≫→

One day, the farmer went to plough his fields.

The students suggest substitutes: one, two or three words that could be rubbed out and others (not necessarily exactly the same number or even consecutively) put in their place.

One day, the farmer went to plough her fields.

One day, the farmer went to see her horses.

One day, the queen went to see her horses race.

And so on.

Unlike **Changing sentences** on page 8, the original structure does not have to be maintained, provided the sentence as a whole remains grammatical.

Acknowledgement: Based on an idea in *Grammar Games* by Mario Rinvolucri (Cambridge University Press, 1984).

Same word, different meanings

Vocabulary expansion through study of homonyms and homophones.

Procedure: Dictate two or three words to your students, each of which has two or more meanings. For instance, *bear*, meaning 'a big animal' or 'to tolerate'. Working in small groups, the students find out and note down as many as they know of the different meanings: they can do this by definition, as in the examples above, or by translation into the mother tongue. If they have dictionaries readily available, you might wish to let them use them. Alternatively, they can simply share what they already know.

You can also use words whose spelling (but not sound) changes with the meaning, for example, *two* and *too*. Then check answers.

Note that words that sound and look the same but have different meanings are *homonyms*; if the spelling and meaning are different, but they sound the same, then they are *homophones*.

The BOX provides examples of both homonyms and homophones, at various levels.

≫→

BOX: Same word, different meanings

Homonyms: elementary

can	like	fire
light	ring	match
room	stick	kind
left	rest	iron
pipe	bank	lie

Homonyms: intermediate

type	capital	case
grave	order	general
wave	cool	bright
cry	miss	land
mind	well	party
beat	mean	patient
box	bear	

Homonyms: advanced

cell	spring	figure
coach	found	long
civil	even	band
board	succeed	conduct
rock	degree	post
sink	concrete	draw

Homophones: elementary

our, hour	to, too, two	I, eye
eight, ate	see, sea	where, wear
be, bee	for, four	sun, son
hear, here	right, write	by, buy
there, their	meet, meat	red, read

Homophones: intermediate

some, sum	not, knot,	accept, except
mail, male	pale, pail	way, weigh
lesson, lessen	night, knight	piece, peace

》》→

D

dear, deer	tale, tail	flour, flower
won, one	oh, owe	week, weak
so, sew		

Homophones: advanced

die, dye	principal, principle	more, moor
hair, hare	current, currant	prey, pray
great, grate	council, counsel	sole, soul
air, heir	morning, mourning	read, reed
him, hymn	waist, waste	toe, tow
site, sight	witch, which	

Say things about a picture

Composing simple grammatical utterances.

Preparation: Do a drawing on the board like one of the pictures in the BOX. Alternatively, simply select a picture from their coursebook, or a magazine picture or poster of your own.

Procedure: The students look at the picture and say things about it; you can give directions that these must be in the form of complete, grammatical sentences, or simply acceptable shorter utterances. For each acceptable contribution write a tick on the board. How many can the class think of in two minutes? Or can they find at least 20 or 30 sentences?

Variation 1: After the first time, students can do the same activity as a group competition: which group can find the most sentences? Or groups can try to beat their own record: can they think of more sentences for a second picture than for the first?

Variation 2: Students think of as many utterances as they can that are obviously *not* true about the picture. Then, optionally, they can correct themselves or each other to form the true statements.

Variation 3: They ask questions whose answers are not obvious from looking at the picture. Write up the more interesting ones on the board, and challenge students to think of creative or original answers.

⟫→

BOX: Say things about a picture

ADAPTED FROM '1000 PICTURES FOR TEACHERS TO COPY' BY ANDREW WRIGHT, COLLINS ELT, 1984.

Search through the book

Quick reading; scanning.

Procedure: Tell the students this is an exercise in quick scanning, a useful study skill. Open your coursebook at random, read out to the students a name, caption or sentence that is prominent on the open page: can they find the place and tell you the page number? You may need to limit the scope ('This is between pages 30 and 50', 'This is somewhere in chapter 5'). Give a little time after you have seen that the quickest student has found it in order to give the others a chance – then ask for the answer. Repeat three or four times.

Variation 1: Don't ask for immediate answers, but get students to write down the page numbers each time – then check results after several 'turns'.

Variation 2: If you do the same thing with a novel, play or short story that the class has been reading, this exercise can also give useful review of the content or plot; whereabouts in the text would they look for the quote, and why?

Variation 3: As an easier variation, using a shorter text (a page or less), ask for the line in which the quoted words appear.

Seeing pictures in your mind

Listening.

Procedure: Ask the students to close their eyes and to sit in as relaxed a way as possible. Say that you are going to describe a picture for them to see in their minds. Describe the picture, slowly, for example:

There are broad fields and in the distance there is a low hill. There are trees on the hill. Above is a great sky filled with clouds. Have a look at the picture for a few moments.

Ask the students to open their eyes and to describe their landscape to their neighbour. Almost certainly they will discover that each saw the landscape differently. Prompt discussion by asking questions, for example:

What could you see in the fields? Was it grass? Was it corn? Were there any animals? How did you feel about the picture?

Note: Some students are quite naturally sensitive about this sort of exercise if they feel that it is being used to conduct some sort of superficial and undignifying analysis of their state of mind. ⟫→

Variation 1: Give the students a description which involves all the senses, not only the visual. For example:

> You are in a room. It is very quiet but you can hear some noises. A clock is ticking. There is the sound of distant traffic, a car going past, a motor bike. You are sitting in a soft, low chair. How do you feel? You would like a drink. You bring the drink to your mouth and take a sip. What is it? Do you like it? Suddenly there is a noise, it's in the house. You stand up.

Once more, ask the students to work with their neighbour. In this variation, say that you will ask the questions and you want each student to give their answers to the question to their neighbour. In your questions, continually invite the students to describe their version of what you sketched out.

Variation 2: Ask the students to close their eyes and listen to a poem or a story: you might like to tell a story over several lessons, just a few minutes each time. The students should relax and see what sort of images come to their minds. They can describe these to their neighbour.

Variation 3: Read a short section of a story or a poem (a paragraph or a stanza) which focusses on a place. The moment you have finished the reading, the students sketch their impression of the place for exactly one minute. The brevity of time ensures an ambiguous drawing with, for example, chairs represented by rectangles. In pairs, the students spend three minutes explaining their drawing and telling each other about what they imagined while hearing the text.

If you want to know more about looking at pictures in the mind, see *How to Improve Your Mind* by Andrew Wright (Cambridge University Press, 1987).

Selling freezers to eskimos

Listening.

Preparation: You will need a picture of an object.

Procedure: Give the picture to a student. Challenge him or her to 'sell' it to the class by arguing why they really need it. This activity can be done seriously or humorously. For example:

> *Student:* (*holding up a picture of a home knitting machine*) We are all tired at the end of the day. We can watch television or we can go to the pub with our friends. But if we go to the

»→

pub every night it costs a lot of money. Knitting is the answer! Knitting is relaxing. We can give the jerseys, etc. to our friends or we can sell them. So we can relax, express ourselves and make money! Who wants one?

The students then decide whether the sales talk was persuasive or not.

Variation 1: Use a word for an object rather than a picture as a stimulus.

Variation 2: Record the sales talks of the students and then use the tape to analyse with them how persuasive they were.

For more ideas on techniques of communicating, including selling, see *How to Communicate Successfully* by Andrew Wright (Cambridge University Press, 1987).

Sentence starters

Writing, speaking and listening.

Procedure: Write on the board:

Being young is …

Ask the students to call out what they think could be added to this sentence beginning. If there is time, ask the students to work with a neighbour, to select four of the lines, put them in order and then to find a fifth line which they feel makes the writing more like a poem. For example:

Being young is being with friends.

Being young is losing friends.

Being young is taking examinations.

Being young is wondering

Whether there will be a future.

⋙→

BOX: Sentence starters

1. Being old is . . .
2. Boredom is . . .
3. Love is . . .
4. A friend is . . .
5. Without you . . .
6. I remember . . .
7. I've forgotten . . .
8. I wish I . . .
9. If I could . . . then I would . . .
10. When I'm 64 I'll . . .

Variation: Dictate the beginning of a sentence. Each student writes it down and then finishes it as he or she wishes.

BOX: Sentence starters (variation)

1. I always feel good when . . .
2. The best time of day is . . .
3. When you live in this country, you should never . . .
4. At midday tomorrow it is fairly certain that . . .
5. Teachers should try very hard to . . .
6. One of the things I should like to know is . . .
7. If I were a millionaire I'd be able to . . .
8. Most people I know seem to be . . .
9. It's a long time since . . .
10. I want to learn English because . . .

Acknowledgement: Based on an idea in *Dictation: New methods, new possibilities* by Paul Davis and Mario Rinvolucri (Cambridge University Press, 1988).

Serial story

Listening comprehension.

Procedure: Using a story that your students can follow easily enough to get enjoyment out of it, read it aloud to the class in instalments – two to five minutes' reading in each lesson. ⟫→

Choose a story with plenty of action, try to stop each time at a moment of suspense – and don't let too much time elapse between instalments!

Silent speech

Pronunciation.

Procedure: In order to focus on pronunciation and the contribution of mouth movement, list on the board words which will illustrate the various sounds you would like to concentrate on.

Tell the class to listen as carefully as they can and then, when you have the students' full attention, 'mouth' a word silently! The students should try to identify the word by carefully watching the movement of your mouth. Ask the students to 'mouth' words for each other derived from the list of words on the board.

Simon says

Listening comprehension.

Procedure: Give the students a series of simple commands to perform:
Stand up!
Open your books!
Put your hands on your head!

Then tell them that only commands prefixed by the words 'Simon says' are to be carried out – anyone who makes a mistake and obeys other commands loses a 'life'. After three or four minutes, how many students have still lost no lives? Or only one?

Variation: Give the command while actually doing an action that may or may not be the same – the students have to do what you say, not (necessarily) what you do.

Slow reveal

Describing and vocabulary review.

Preparation: You will need a picture large enough for the class to see.

Procedure: Put the picture behind a piece of paper or in a large envelope. Reveal the picture in stages. At each stage, ask the class to

⟫→

identify what they can see and what the whole picture might be. Encourage differences of opinion and promote discussion.

Variation: A text can be used instead of a picture on an overhead projector. The transparency can be covered by a piece of paper.

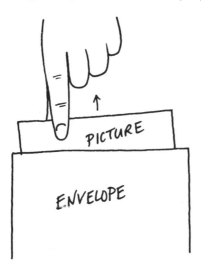

Something interesting about myself

Talking; volunteering personal information.

Procedure: A volunteer student tells the others something interesting about him or herself which he or she is willing to talk about.

I play in a jazz band.
My family is going to live abroad.

The others ask questions.

It is a good idea to start the ball rolling by being the first volunteer yourself; or ask students who you know are more confident and uninhibited to be the first.

Songs

Listening, reading and singing.

Preparation: Select a tape recording of a song, or learn a song so that you can sing it. Prepare an overhead transparency (or a poster, or a handout) of the words of the song. ⟫➔

E

Procedure: Play the song on the tape (or sing it yourself). Show the words of the song and ask the students to follow the words and to sing while you play it again. Deal with any questions or confusion over meaning.

Play the song again when you have another five minutes, and help the students to learn it.

Variation 1: Before playing the song, write on the board a selection of words and phrases from the song which you think will point to the meaning of the song. Ask the students to copy the words down, and then ask them what they think the song will be about. Play the song and ask the students to tick off the words as they hear them.

Variation 2: Ask the students to choose a phrase in the song which they like and would like to remember.

Variation 3: Give the students the text of the song with gaps in it. The gaps can be every tenth word or, perhaps more usefully, about ten lexical or grammatical features (in a two or-three minute song) which you would like them to focus on. Play the song several times until the students, working in pairs, have completed their text.

Variation 4: Give out a complete text in which some of the words are wrong. The students listen and correct the text.

Variation 5: Ask students to mime the characters and storyline of the song. Some songs (mainly intended for children) are designed for this purpose, for example, 'Heads and shoulders, knees and toes'.

Note: Adults can sometimes be persuaded to learn these 'mime songs' if you point out how useful it would be to be able to do them if they ever stay with an English-speaking family with children.

Variation 6: Ask the students to draw an expressive line while they listen to the song and then to explain it to their neighbour. Example:

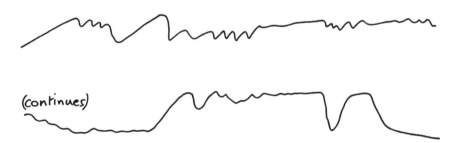

(continues)

Spelling bee

Spelling.

Procedure: Dictate ten words the students may have difficulty spelling, or that you have recently taught. The students write them down. You may wish the students to help each other, compare results and decide which spelling they think is right, before giving the correct answers.

Note any words that students have particular difficulties with, and review them later.

Some words which are often mis-spelt are suggested in the BOX.

Variation: In order to improve the learning value of this activity, briefly review the correct spellings before dictating the words.

BOX: Spelling bee

Elementary

quiet	address	water
altogether	beginning	write
chocolate	bicycle	always
two	eye	right
young	answer	believe
house	fruit	clothes
where	almost	question
friend	beautiful	daughter
sea	enough	people
business	colo(u)r	thief
already	vegetable	because
chief	money	cupboard
light	knee	

Intermediate

straight	scene	international
design	echo	symbol
independent	except	tongue
accident	profession	obvious
advantage	measure	except
accept	headache	advertisement
laugh	stomach	guarantee
pleasure	parallel	scientist

⟫→

---

responsible	murder	anxious
success	appear(ance)	microscope
calm	treasure	embarrassed
casualty	religious	ceiling
patient	knowledge	character
geography	laboratory	height
foreign	efficient	psychology
assess	rough	jealous
assignment	sympathise	average
ghost	comfortable	communicate
suggest	persuade	conscience
necessary	weight	dumb
privilege	congratulations	discipline
cough	technician	criticism

Advanced

prologue	dialogue	abbreviate
comprehensible	seize	abdomen
yacht	tyranny	miniature
pronunciation	agriculture	martyr
amateur	unique	rhetorical
manoeuvre	ambiguous	syllable
genuine	diaphragm	analysis
appreciate	weird	chasm
principle	archaic	paralyse
asphalt	sophisticated	rhythm
authentic	hygiene	genesis
bourgeois	bronchitis	bureaucracy
catastrophe	colleague	rheumatism
hypochondriac	courageous	encyclop(a)edia

Stories

Listening comprehension; talking.

Procedure: Tell a short story or relate an experience to your class; it could be something that happened to you personally, that you read in

»→

80

the paper, heard on the radio, saw on television; or an event of local interest.

Note that even if the students are familiar with the story – for example, if they saw the television programme you are describing – they will still usually enjoy and benefit from hearing your account.

Variation 1: Enrich your story-telling by the use of a picture, or pictures; by using furniture to represent items in the narrative; by the use of mime. Very simple sketching on the board can also add a great deal: the following series, for example, could illustrate an account of a teacher's visit to Africa to teach English:

Variation 2: The 'story' can also be a description of a person you know, a place you like, or something you enjoy or hate doing.

Variation 3: Students react to and discuss your account, and contribute stories of their own.

The disappearing text

Reading and speaking.

Procedure: If you have written a text on the board and no longer need it, erase a small part of it, not more than one or two lines. Ask a student to read out the text on the board to the rest of the class and to include the missing words from memory.

Erase one or two more words. Ask another student to read the text on the board and to include the missing words.

Continue in this way until the whole text has been erased and remembered.

Acknowledgement: We first came across this elegant and economical idea in a workshop given by Michael Buckby in 1973.

The most

Superlatives.

Procedure: Give, or ask students to suggest, a group of six or seven
items linked to a common subject area, for example, names of
animals. The students try to define each as 'the most . . . ' or 'the -est'
of the group. If the items were horse, elephant, spider, cobra, parrot,
dog, they might say:

The horse is the fastest.
The dog is the friendliest.
The cobra is the most dangerous, etc.

Other possible subject areas: food, clothes, famous people, furniture,
household items.

The other you

Describing.

Procedure: Tell the students that you will ask some questions and that
you want them to answer by pretending to be the sort of person they
would like to be.

Give the students a minute to imagine the kind of person they would
like to be. They can do this seriously or humorously. You then ask the
questions, but students should give their answers to their neighbour.
Examples of questions are given in the BOX opposite.

Variation 1: Students can ask the questions either of their neighbour or
of the class as a whole. Answers can be given to one neighbour, to a
group or to the class.

Variation 2: If you think the students would like the idea, help them to
establish this 'other you' character and offer other short activities in
future lessons which allow them to develop the character further. For
example, you can mention a current event in the news and ask how
their other character would respond to it.

Variation 3: The students take on the role of the sort of person they feel
is the opposite of themselves, perhaps an utterly crazy character if they
are normally sane and sensible, or a cool and tough character if they
are normally warm and easy-going.

⟫→

BOX: The other you

1. Are you a man or a woman?
2. How old are you?
3. What is your name?
4. What job do you do?
5. If you won a million pounds, what would you do?
6. What do you want in life?
7. What do you worry about?
8. What are your main problems?
9. What makes you happy?
10. How do you get on with other people?

Three-picture story

Oral fluency and imagination.

Preparation: Select three magazine pictures which are large enough to be seen by the whole class. The first one should show one or two people in a setting. The second and third ones should be of an object, a situation or an event. The second and third ones do not need to show the people in the first picture.

Procedure: Display the first picture. Ask the students to call out anything they want to say about it. Your role is to stimulate observation and invention and then to gather the suggestions and to put them into story form. As the students offer more ideas, you add them to the story, continually retelling it from the beginning. After a few moments, you can display the second picture and later the third. As you see your five minutes coming to an end, ask the students to suggest a conclusion. Try to retell the completed story before the time is up. This is an example of how the story might begin:

> You: (*Showing the first picture*) What do you want to tell me about the picture?
> Student: There are two people.
> You: Yes. Anything else?
> Student: It's a man and a woman. They are lovers.
> You: What are their names?
> Student: James and Samantha.
> You: Good. Where are they? What time is it?

⟫→

Student:	It's evening. It's dark. It's perhaps in the country or a park.
You:	What shall we say?
Student:	The country.
You:	(*Assuming a story-telling style*) Well, it was late in the evening. James and Samantha didn't know where they were; it was so dark. They thought they must be in the country.
You:	(*Showing the second picture*) What do you want to tell me about this picture?
Student:	It's a car. It's going very quickly.
You:	It was late in the evening. James and Samantha didn't know where they were, it was so dark. They thought they must be in the country. Suddenly they saw a car. It was travelling very quickly, etc.

Tongue twisters

Pronunciation.

Procedure: Write a tongue twister on the board, and read it with the students slowly at first, then faster. Make sure the students' pronunciation is acceptable. Then individual volunteers try to say it quickly three times. See the BOX for some examples of tongue twisters.

BOX: Tongue twisters

She sells sea shells on the sea shore.

Mixed biscuits, mixed biscuits.

Red leather, yellow leather, red leather, yellow leather.

A proper copper coffee pot.

Three grey geese in a green field grazing.

Swan swam over the pond, swim swan swim; swan swam back again – well swum swan!

Peter Piper picked a peck of pickled pepper.
Did Peter Piper pick a peck of pickled pepper?
If Peter Piper picked a peck of pickled pepper,
Where's the peck of pickled pepper Peter Piper picked?

Unusual view

Vocabulary review.

Procedure: Draw a familiar object from an unusual point of view, for example, a rectangle representing the top of a table. Ask the students to identify it. Encourage different opinions.

Note: To ensure that all the students are active, ask them to tell their neighbour what they think it is before inviting a class discussion. You might like to make use of 'could' in your responses. For example:

    You: What is it?
  Student: A window.
    You: It could be but it isn't.   etc.

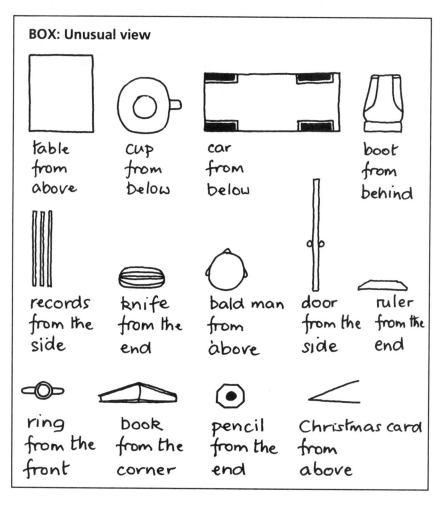

BOX: Unusual view

table from above

cup from below

car from below

boot from behind

records from the side

knife from the end

bald man from above

door from the side

ruler from the end

ring from the front

book from the corner

pencil from the end

Christmas card from above

Use the dictionary

Practice in dictionary use, for classes where all the students have dictionaries – either monolingual or bilingual.

Procedure: Give a set of six to ten English words the students probably do not know yet. They find out the meanings of as many as they can from the dictionary within a given time: three minutes, for example. Check the meanings.

This activity can be used to prepare the vocabulary they are going to meet in their next reading passage.

Vocabulary steps

Vocabulary review.

Procedure: Draw a series of steps on the board. Write 'warm' on a middle step. Ask the students to suggest words they could write on the other steps which are warmer or colder than the word 'warm'. The students can use a Thesaurus, if they have one.

»→

Variation 1: Take any set of concepts which can be graded objectively. For example, metals can be graded according to value.

VALUE BY WEIGHT

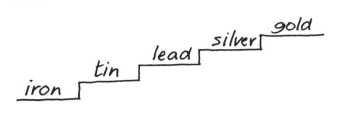

Variation 2: Take any set of concepts which can only be graded by subjective criteria. For example, animals can be graded according to how dangerous they are. Would you agree with the grading in the examples below?

DIFFERENT VIEWS OF THE DANGER POTENTIAL OF CREATURES

mosquito
cobra
tiger
bull
dog
spider

tiger
cobra
bull
dog
mosquito
spider

Variation 3: Tell the students to write down one sentence for each word. Each sentence should illustrate the relative intensity or ranking of the word. In this activity it is helpful if the words are listed vertically in order. Then the sentence can be written opposite each word.

Acknowledgement: The above variation is based on an activity described in a contribution by Tessa Woodward in *The Recipe Book*, edited by Seth Lindstromberg (Pilgrims Longman, 1990).

⋙→

BOX: Vocabulary steps

Beginners to intermediate

(temperature)   cold, cool, warm, hot

(size)   tiny, small, big, enormous

(quality)   worst, worse, bad, good, better, best

(happiness)   miserable, sad, unhappy, happy

(speed)   legs, bicycle, bus, car, train, plane

Intermediate to advanced

(date of invention)   taps (ancient Egypt), scissors (ancient Greece), glass
  mirror (1300), steam car (1771), balloon (1782), steam train (1800),
  photograph (1826), bicycle with pedals (1839), petrol car (1885)

(size)   minute, tiny, small, big, huge, gigantic, immense, vast

(calories)   lemon (10), orange (40), boiled egg (80), banana (85), fried egg
  (125), bag of chips (250), slice of apple pie (300)

(frequency)   rarely, occasionally, sometimes, often, frequently

(speed)   walking, jogging, running, sprinting

(liking)   appreciate, be charmed by, like, care for, cherish, love, adore

Walking warmers

Listening and acting.

Procedure: You need a space free from chairs and tables. Use a selection
of activities, each lasting about 10 to 15 seconds, to build up a five-
minute period. See the BOX.

Note: These activities are potential 'warmers' for new classes and for
classes in which the students know each other. The physical movement
and the inventiveness can provide a welcome change from more
sedentary work. The examples in the BOX are divided into those which
involve the students as individuals and those which invite the students
to relate to each other.

Variation: Ask the students to invent their own actions and to take the
role of organiser.

⟫→

BOX: Walking warmers

As individuals

Tell the students to walk about:
- as if they are exhausted
- as if they have just heard some wonderful news
- as if they are carrying a heavy suitcase
- as if it is bitterly cold
- as if they don't want to be seen
- as if they are a little child
- as if they are very old
- as if they are ten feet tall
- as if they are walking on ice
- as if they are sleepwalking
- as if they are a king or queen walking to the coronation
- as if they are crossing a stream on stepping stones
- as if they are a beggar
- as if they have stolen goods on their person
- as if they are walking on a tightrope

Relating to others

- nodding and smiling at each other
- greeting each other in a familiar way perhaps by shaking hands and slapping each other on the shoulder
- greeting each other as if they have not seen each other for a long time
- behaving towards each other as if the other person was offensive the last time they met
- behaving as if they do not really like each other
- behaving as though the other person is deaf
- behaving as if the other person has bad breath
- behaving as though they think the other person is stupid
- behaving as though they think the other person is dangerous
- behaving as though the other person is an extremely distinguished and elderly person
- greeting each other and saying anything which comes into their heads

We both . . .

Getting to know each other; use of *both* and *neither*.

Procedure: In pairs, students ask each other questions in order to find as many things as they can that they have in common. They are not allowed to use ideas that are immediately apparent through looking at each other, for example, 'We are both tall.' They must discover them through talking. After two or three minutes, invite pairs to tell the class some of their results. Sentences will tend to be of the form: 'We both . . .' or 'Neither of us . . .'

Note: The grammar of sentences using *We both* . . . is a little tricky. Normally the two words go together:

We both play the piano.

But if there is an auxiliary verb like *is* or *can*, then the word *both* is normally after it and before the main verb.

We can both play the piano.

The phrase *neither of us* should be followed by a singular verb, except in very informal style.

What are they talking about?

Composing sentences in the present.

Procedure: Write a sentence on the board in inverted commas; this represents a bit of conversation that has been overheard (there are some examples in the BOX). The students guess what the person is talking about and anything else they can infer about the situation – for example, what sort of person the speaker is, what the relationship is between the speaker and the person addressed, and so on.

You might decide in advance what the 'right' answer is; or try to come to a class consensus; or find as many possible 'solutions' as possible.

Variation: The students' solutions can be presented through dramatisation: the students act through the situation in which the utterance occurred.

Acknowledgement: Based on *Variations on a theme* by Alan Maley and Alan Duff (Cambridge University Press, 1978).

》》→

> **BOX: What are they talking about?**
>
> 1. 'You idiot! We'll never get it back now!'
> 2. 'It's awful! Let's ask for our money back!'
> 3. 'You can't? Well, we'll just have to manage without.'
> 4. 'She's far too big, we'll never get her in.'
> 5. 'It's stuck – could you give me a hand?'
> 6. 'I don't approve, but if you must, you must.'
> 7. 'Found it at last! But it's too late now.'
> 8. 'I can't afford to, after what John's done . . . '
> 9. 'Just in time! You've saved us! In another minute . . . '
> 10. 'You should have thought of that before. Nothing I can do now.'

What did they say?

Indirect speech.

Procedure: Towards the end of the lesson, challenge students to recall things that have been said by the teacher or students during the course of the lesson – but they must report them in indirect speech. For example:

> Andreas said he was sorry he was late.
> You asked us if we had found the homework difficult.

See if they can remember 10, 12 or 15 things that were said; if there is time, write them up on the board.

Variation 1: Use the same activity as the follow-up to any listening activity as a way of reviewing the text.

Variation 2: After a discussion, you try to recall things the students have said. They remind you of ones you have forgotten.

What has just happened?

Use of the present perfect to describe something that has just happened.

Procedure: Write a series of exclamations on the board – not more than about ten (there is a selection to choose from in the BOX). In pairs or groups, students choose an exclamation, think of an event which might have caused someone to say it, and write down a brief

⟫→

description of the event, using the present perfect. For example, they might choose 'What?', and write:

Someone hasn't heard clearly what was just said.

Then they choose another and do the same again. After two minutes, invite students to read out their sentences without identifying the exclamations that gave rise to them; the rest of the class guess what the exclamations were.

BOX: What has just happened?

Oh!	Oh?	Congratulations!
I'm sorry!	Great!	What?
No!	Thanks!	Welcome!
Never mind!	It's a deal!	Hello?
Goodbye!	Thank goodness!	Yes, of course!
Ow!	Bad luck!	Great!

What might you do with it?

Simple sentences using *might* or *could.*

Procedure: One or two students stand with their backs to the board; they are the guessers. You write on the board the name of a well-known household object: for example, a pencil, a cup, or a box of matches. The rest of the class help the guessers to find out what the object is by suggesting things they might (or could) do with it. They should use their imaginations, and not give away the answer by suggesting the obvious use – at least, not immediately! For example, if the object is a pencil, they could say things like:

I could pick it up.
I might throw it at someone.
I might point at something with it.
I could scratch my head with it.

Note that in this case *might* and *could* are used interchangeably.

What's the explanation?

Asking questions.

Procedure: Describe to the students a brief situation or event which

⇶→

92

seems on the face of it strange or inexplicable. They ask questions in order to find out what the true explanation is. For example:

> The man had been a hostage for ten years. His wife watched him leave the plane, and called to him excitedly. He did not respond.

Through the answers to 'narrowing-down' questions ('Could the man hear her?', 'Was he deaf?', etc.), the students should be able to discover that the woman saw her husband on television.

There are further examples in the BOX.

Students may not be able to reach some of the more far-fetched answers on their own – you may need to supply hints. Remember that the aim is to get them to guess the answers successfully, not to frustrate them!

BOX: What's the explanation?

1 The man had been a hostage for ten years. His wife watched him leave the plane, and called to him excitedly. He did not respond.

2. The woman had a blackout for a minute and fell backwards into a deep hole. She was not hurt.

3. It was late at night. 'I love you', he said, kissing her. 'I love you too, darling', she responded. Then her husband walked in. What do you think happened next?

4. The man was injected with a deadly poison – but it did not kill him.

5. She was enjoying a swim when she suddenly felt something in her mouth and, scared, came out of the water fast.

6. 'I'll marry you', she promised him. But I knew it was not to be. How?

7. 'Go away!' he said. This made her very happy.

8. The walls of the house were damp. But she assured me they would not go mouldy. She was right.

9. Everyone around him knew who he was; but no one knew his name.

10. She made an injection in my arm and drew out some blood. But I knew the results would do me no good.

Answers: 1. She saw him on television.   2. It happened while she was scuba-diving in deep water.   3. The husband helped his wife to put their small son to bed.   4. He was already dead.   5. She was a fish.   6. I had seen the film before.   7. It was the first time he had spoken after weeks in a coma following an accident.   8. The house was an igloo.   9. He had just been born.   10. She was a mosquito.

What's the story behind it?

Questions and answers.

Procedure: Show the students an object which belongs to you, for example, a penknife, a bracelet, your jacket. Tell the class about the object and encourage the students to ask you questions.

Ask individual students if they would mind telling you the story behind an object of their own.

Where did it come from?

Vocabulary review and discussion.

Procedure: Write the name of an artefact in the middle of the board. Ask the students to say what it is made of or other questions designed to establish what the object or material was like in its previous state. Each time they suggest something, write it on the board and then repeat the question. For example, starting with the word 'shoe':

    You: Shoe. What's it made of?
Student: Leather.
    You: Right . . . where does leather come from?
Student: From a cow.
    You: And what does a cow live on?   etc.

leather   cotton   rubber
cow   cotton plant   tree
grass   field
     earth
     old plants
     mud
     river
     rocks
     mountains

Who, where and what?

Describing and guessing.

Procedure: Describe an object in the classroom, and at the end of the description ask, 'What is it?' Follow this with a description of a person who is known to the students. They must try to identify what or who you have described.

> *You:* It's got two doors, it's green and I keep books in it.
> *Student:* The cupboard.
> *You:* She's wearing a mauve jersey and she's sitting in the middle of the room.
> *Student:* Wendy.

Once the activity has become understood, individual students describe people, places or objects for the rest of the class to identify.

Variation: Having introduced the activity by your demonstration of it, divide the class into two. Choose a student and whisper to him or her the name of an object, person, place or event. The student must then describe the object, person, place or event so well that his or her half of the class can identify it. Repeat this with the other half of the class. Let the two halves of the class continue to take turns and see which half of the class recognises the most descriptions.

Why have you got a monkey in your bag?

Imaginative questions and answers.

Procedure: Empty a bag – yours or one of the students'. Go up to one of the students, give him or her the bag and ask:

Why have you got a monkey in your bag?

The student has to think of a convincing or original reason why there is a monkey in his or her bag. After giving the reason and answering any questions from the rest of the class, he or she then takes the bag and goes up to another student with the same question, only this time using another object, for example:

Why have you got an axe in your bag?

And so on.

This is a good activity for lighthearted relaxation: after exams, for example, or at the end of term.

Why might you . . . ?

Conditionals.

Procedure: Suggest an unlikely action, and ask the students if they can imagine under what circumstances they might do it. You may or may not wish to instruct them to make full conditional sentences. For example:

Why might you stand on your head?

Possible answers:

If I were performing in a circus, I might stand on my head.
If I wanted to look at something upside down . . .

See the BOX for other possible examples.

BOX: Why might you?

1. . . . go to live in another country?
2. . . . stop talking for a day?
3. . . . eat a piece of paper?
4. . . . dye your hair green?
5. . . . go and live in a tree?
6. . . . ride an elephant?
7. . . . sleep all day?
8. . . . jump out of the window?
9. . . . visit the Prime Minister/President?
10. . . . refuse to come to this lesson?

Word cards

Constructing sentences.

Preparation: For this activity you will need thick felt tip pens and strips of paper or card. The simplest way of preparing the strips is to tear or cut A4 paper into four strips. (Wonderful sources of strips of card are local printers, who may not charge you for them.)

If you have time, write the words on the strips beforehand, one word per strip. Alternatively, the students do this for you. The words can be taken from sentences in your coursebook. Ensure that there is a reasonable balance of words so that a variety of sentences can be built up with them. ⟫→

A fast way of doing this is to take one sentence from the coursebook and then to add alternative words for the different parts of the sentence.

You need between five and 15 word cards.

Procedure: Students take it in turns to come to the front of the class and to stand facing the class showing their word card. Succeeding students should stand with the other students so that their words begin to make up a sentence. As a sentence begins to emerge, it may be that students displaying their words have to move further along or further back in the sentence. This is an activity which provides an intense experience of sentence construction and in a form which many students can appreciate.

You might like to give out some blank cards. The students with blank cards can stand in any position and be any word which makes the sentence complete.

Variation: Write a word on a strip which you know could be the first word in a sentence. Challenge a student to imagine what word might come next and to write it on a strip and stand in line at the front. Even when the sentence is complete, students can add words to the sentence, for example, adverbs or adjectives. Students can also attempt to substitute words, for example, pronouns for nouns; the student with the noun must sit down. The aim for the students is to be at the front and within the sentence at the end of the activity. For example:

Words beginning with . . .

Vocabulary, spelling.

Procedure: Give a letter, and ask the students to write down as many
words as they can that begin with it in two minutes. They can do this
individually, or in pairs or small groups. Then they tell you what their
words are, and you write them up on the board. Encourage students
to ask for explanations of words that any of them did not know.

Note: It is a good idea at the writing-up stage to have an aim: can we all
together get 20, or 30, or 40 words?

Variation: Ask students to think of words that *end* with a certain letter,
or – much easier, for elementary classes – that simply include it.

Words out of . . .

Vocabulary, spelling.

Procedure: Write up a selection of about ten disconnected letters
scattered on the board, and ask students to use them to make words.
Each letter may be used only once in each word. Make sure there are
two or three vowels among them! For example:

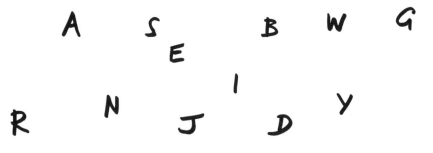

Students might suggest words like: grain, beg, angry, yes, begin. They
can suggest the words directly to you to be written up immediately, or
spend two or three minutes thinking of suggestions (individually, or
in pairs or small groups) before pooling. As in **Words beginning
with** . . . above, it is a good idea to aim to reach a certain number of
words: 20, say, or more.

If you prefer to use long words as the source for eliciting short ones,
then some possible words are: international, dictionary, systematic,
beautiful, democratic, agriculture, unbelievable, transformation,
archaeology. ⟫→

Variation 1: Give only six or seven letters, but allow students to use letters more than once in a single word.

Variation 2: At the beginning, invite students to suggest the letters. Just make sure that these include vowels!

Variation 3: Give the students two or three minutes to think of words. Then they come together in groups or the full class, sharing their lists. Any words that more than one student has thought of are crossed out. Who has the longest list of 'unique' words?

Would you make a good witness?

Description.

Preparation: Choose a picture of a scene which is large enough to be seen by the whole class. The picture should show people and objects in a setting; a street scene would be ideal. If you haven't got a picture like this, then any picture will do.

Procedure: Provoke the students in a playful manner, saying you will find out if they have good memories. Then show the class the picture for two minutes. If the class is big, you might have to do this by walking up and down the aisles showing the picture from side to side. Turn the picture away from the class, so that only you can see it. Ask the students what they can remember. Do not confirm or reject ideas. Encourage differences of opinion to raise interest. Finally, show the picture again.

Variation: Show the picture and then ask the students to write down what they remember about it and, having done so, to compare their list with their neighbour's.

Wrangling

Learning and repeating dialogues.

Procedure: Choose a dialogue consisting of two short sentences expressing disagreement. For example:

I'm sure it's going to rain.
Of course it isn't.

Two volunteer students say their sentences to each other, as an argument: they are allowed to use only the words of the text, but must vary

》→

99

stress, gesture and tone to try to convince each other! The first to give up is the loser.

You may wish to use a text from your coursebook as a basis for the dialogue, in order to review vocabulary or grammar.

Other possible dialogues are in the BOX.

Variation 1: Allow students to improvise variations or a continuation, developing the exercise into a role play. In the above dialogue, for example, the pair could decide what it is that makes them concerned about the weather (are they planning a picnic? or a walk?) and develop a discussion about why they think it will or will not rain, and what they might do if it does, etc.

Variation 2: The dialogues may also be used as a basis for discussion, as in **What are they talking about?** on page 90.

BOX: Wrangling

1. 'Still, I think you'd better tell them!'
   'Oh, no, they'll kill me!'

2. 'It's cold. Don't you want to come in?'
   'No, I'm quite happy out here.'

3. 'I'm really having a lovely time.'
   'Well, you don't look like it.'

4. 'The answer is no.'
   'By why? It's not fair.'

5. 'It's late, there's no time. Let's go.'
   'But I haven't had breakfast yet!'

6. 'I don't want to hear any excuses. You're fired!'
   'But I can explain. Please let me explain!'

You write next!

Brief writing practice.

Procedure: Each student has a sheet of paper, at the top of which he or she writes a sentence: it can be a simple statement of fact or opinion, or a question. For example:

What are you going to do after the lesson?

or:

It's very cold today.

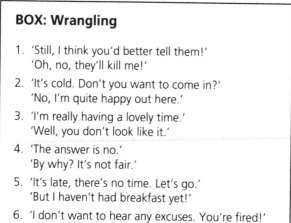

or:

I hate people smoking near me.

This is then passed to a neighbour, who adds an answer, comment or further question (again, in the form of a full sentence) and passes it on to someone else. And so on. The paper is not folded, so that all previous contributions are visible to each writer.

After about five contributions, students are invited to read out the results; these are often amusing!

The activity can, of course, be done in pairs rather than by individuals.

Acknowledgement: Based on an idea by Ephraim Weintraub.

Bibliography

The books below all contain a range of excellent activities, some of which are estimated to take 15 minutes or less.

Baudains, Marjorie and Baudains, Richard, *Alternatives*, Longman, 1990.

Carrier, Michael, *Take 5: Games and activities for the language teacher*, Nelson, 1985.

Davis, Paul, and Rinvolucri, Mario, *Dictation*, Cambridge University Press, 1988.

Davis, Paul, and Rinvolucri, Mario, *The Confidence Book*, Pilgrims Longman, 1990.

Frank, Christine and Rinvolucri, Mario, *Grammar in Action*, Pergamon Press, 1983.

Greenall, Simon, *Language Games and Activities*, Stanley Thornes Ltd, 1984.

Klippel, Friederike, *Keep Talking*, Cambridge University Press, 1984.

Lee, W. R., *Language Teaching Games and Contests*, Oxford University Press, 1979.

Lindstromberg, Seth, (ed.), *The Recipe Book*, Pilgrims Longman, 1990.

Maley, Alan, and Duff, Alan, *Drama Techniques in Language Learning*, Cambridge University Press, 1978.

Morgan, John, and Rinvolucri, Mario, *Vocabulary*, Oxford University Press, 1986.

Nolasco, Rob, and Arthur, Lois, *Conversation*, Oxford University Press, 1987.

Ur, Penny, *Discussions that Work*, Cambridge University Press, 1981.

Ur, Penny, *Teaching Listening Comprehension*, Cambridge University Press, 1984.

Ur, Penny, *Grammar Practice Activities*, Cambridge University Press, 1988.

Wright, Andrew, *Games for Language Learning*, Cambridge University Press, 1984.

Wright, Andrew, *How to Be Entertaining*, Cambridge University Press, 1986.

Wright, Andrew, *How to Improve Your Mind*, Cambridge University Press, 1987.

Wright, Andrew, *How to Communicate Successfully*, Cambridge University Press, 1987.

Wright, Andrew, *Pictures for Language Learning*, Cambridge University Press, 1989.

Index

Since titles of activities are arranged in alphabetical order in the book, they are not listed in this index. Please look them up in the Contents on pages vi–viii.

feelings (*cont.*)
    dislikes, 45–6; Seeing pictures in your
    mind, 72–3

general knowledge, **Amazing facts, 2;**
    General knowledge, 30–3
grammar, see *sentence structure*; for
    specific structures, see under the
    name of the structure
grammar mistakes, **Correcting**
    mistakes, 10–12
guessing, **Abstract picture, 1;**
    Ambiguous picture, 3; Damaged
    property, 14–15; Feel the object, 26;
    Flashing, 29–30; Guessing, 34;
    Miming, 51–2; Slow reveal, 76–7;
    Unusual view, 85; What are they
    talking about?, 90–1; What's the
    explanation, 92–3; Who, where and
    what?, 95

have (got), **Detectives** (variation), 16
homonyms, homophones, **Same word,**
    different meanings, 68–70

ice-breakers, see *warm-ups*
indirect speech, **What did they say?,**
    91
integration of activities into lesson,
    Introduction, xi–xii
interpreting, **What are they talking**
    about?, 90–1
interrogative, see *asking questions*, or
    guessing
interviewing, **Interview an interesting**
    personality, 39
intonation, **It was the way she said it,**
    42

journals, **Diaries, 17**

learning value, **Introduction, x–xi**
lecture (mini-), **Amazing facts, 2;**
    Express your view, 23; Selling
    freezers to eskimos, 73–4; What's the
    story behind it?, 94
lessons, feedback on, **Discussing**
    lessons, 17–18

level of activities, **Introduction, xi**
listening, **Amazing facts, 2, Categories,**
    6–7; Hearing mistakes, 34; I'm
    pulling your leg, 38; Interrupting the
    story, 39; Magical entertainment,
    46–7; Oral cloze, 61; Picture
    dictation, 61; Relaxation technique,
    67; Seeing pictures in your mind,
    72–3; Serial story, 75–6; Simon says,
    76; Songs, 77–8; Walking warmers,
    88–9
loan words, **English words in our**
    language, 20
lotto, see *bingo*

memory games, see *recalling*
mime, **Miming, 51–2; Miming adverbs,**
    52
mistakes, **Correcting mistakes, 10–12**
modals, **Evidence, 20–1; What might**
    you do with it?, 92
morphology, **Prefixes and suffixes,**
    62–3

narrative, see *stories*
negation, **Detectives, 16; Don't say yes**
    or no, 19
neither, see *both*
news, **Expanding headlines, 22**
numbers, **Dictate numbers, 17; First,**
    second, third, 28; Numbers in my
    life, 58

passive, **Damaged property, 14–15**
past tenses, **Chain story, 7; Damaged**
    property (mainly questions in the
    past), 14–15; **Detectives, 16;**
    Listening to sounds, 46; Three-
    picture story, 83–4; Would you make
    a good witness?, 99
pictures, activities using, **Abstract**
    picture, 1; Ambiguous picture, 3;
    Draw a word, 19; Flashing, 29–30;
    Imaginative descriptions, 36–7;
    Picture dictation, 61; Say things
    about a picture, 70–1; Slow reveal,
    76–7; Three-picture story, 83–4;
    Unusual view, 85

104